Scribes of Speculative Fiction II

By
Cristopher DeRose

SCRIBES OF SPECULATIVE FICTION II

Scribes of Speculative Fiction II
By Cristopher DeRose
© 2015, BearManor Media All Rights Reserved.
No part of this book may be reproduced in any form or by any means, electronic, mechanical, digital, photocopying or recording, except for the inclusion in a review, without permission in writing from the publisher.

Published in the USA by:
BearManor Media
P O Box 71426
Albany, Georgia 31708
www.bearmanormedia.com

ISBN: 978-1-59393-784-3
Printed in the United States of America
Cover concept by Ryan DeRose
Book design by Robbie Adkins, www.adkinsconsult.com

Dedicated to the life of my Mom, Lois,
which means "woman warrior."

Table of Contents

Raymond Benson 1
Weston Ochse 6
Jack Ketchum 11
Raymond Feist 14
Scott Leberecht, Ed Sanchez, and Matt Compton 17
Joe Schreiber 22
Caitlin R. Kiernan 26
William Nolan 32
Nancy Holder 35
Tad Williams 39
Kathe Koja 43
Tom Piccirilli 49
Kevin J. Anderson 54
Storm Constantine 58
Darrell Schweitzer 63
Brian Hodge 68
Paul Di Filippo 78
Steve Rasnic Tem 83
Norman Prentiss 88
Nancy Kress 96
Mike Resnick 99
Donna Burgess 105
Roger Price 109
Charles De Lint 114
Sandy DeLuca 118
Nancy Kilpatrick 121

RAYMOND BENSON

Raymond Benson may be best known as the fourth official author of the James Bond novels. Including adaptations of *Die Another Day* and *The World Is Not Enough*, and the authoritative non-fiction book, *The James Bond Bedside Companion*, but what is just as much testimony to his talent is the fact he is an accomplished musician, video game designer and director of stage productions.

His work outside the Bond franchise has included the *Black Stiletto* book series as well as numerous mysteries and thrillers such as *A Hard Day's Death, Sweetie's Diamonds* and *Torment*. As a Bond and an overall spy genre nut, it was with great pleasure that I was able to conduct this interview.

You can find Raymond online at: raymondbenson.com

Q: How were you approached to take over the literary part of the Bond franchise?

A: I had written *The James Bond Bedside Companion* in the 80s. When I was researching the book, I went to England and met members of Ian Fleming's family, his business people, friends, etc. The copyright holders liked the book when it came out and we stayed in touch. I did little odd jobs for them (no pun intended) in the late 80s and early 90s. Then, when John Gardner announced that he would no longer continue writing the books in 1995, they simply asked me if I'd like to give it a shot.

Q: Did you have any trepidation about writing new adventures?

A: I was stepping into very big shoes! Anyone who didn't have trepidations would need his head examined.

Q: John Gardner seems to have taken a lot of flak over how he reinterpreted Bond during his run as author of the franchise. Do you feel some of the heavy-handed criticism was warranted by the fanbase?

A: It's a large fan base and therefore very opinionated, just as any big franchise fan base is (*Star Wars, Star Trek, Batman*, etc.). You can't please everyone. Every fan has his or her own interpretation of the character in one's head. Bond comes with a lot of baggage. John had his fans and his detractors. I had my fans and detractors. The same is true for the authors who came after me. Even Ian Fleming had his detractors!

Q: How much interaction did you have with the filmmakers of the Bond films?

A: Not much. Only when I was writing the film novelizations did I work with EON. I went to Pinewood Studios to see the sets and costumes and designs for the gadgets, but saw no filming. I communicated with the screenwriters. The original novels, though, were just between me and Ian Fleming Publications.

Q: Did you have a particular Bond in mind when you were writing the books?

A: The one that I pictured in my head when I first read the Fleming novels back in the 60s, and it wasn't Sean Connery! I'd say he resembled the John McClusky drawings in the Daily Express comics, but that was before I'd even seen those comics. Every reader imagines his/her own Bond in the part as they read......I had fans tell me "I could hear Sean Connery say those lines!" or "I could hear Pierce Brosnan say those lines!" That's good. When a reader can inject his/her own Bond into the story, then I've succeeded.

Q: Which book of yours do you feel really captured the dynamic of James Bond?

A: I would like to think they all did!

Q: What should the next direction be for the Bond novels?

A: That's not for me to say. I had my seven-year tenure, I wrote six original books, three movie novelizations, and three short stories. That's a pretty good run. I don't own the character and therefore have no say in what Ian Fleming Publications decides to do with the franchise.

Q: What do you think of Daniel Craig as 007?

A: I think he's terrific!

Q: What can we expect to see in the re-issue of the *Bond Bedside Companion?*

A: It's the same book as before. I've written a new Introduction, explaining why I can't and won't update it, but I give a brief rundown of what has happened in the Bond world between 1988 and the present.

Q: Will there be any more *Splinter Cell* novels to follow?

A: Not from me.

Q: What was it like to work with John Milius for *Homefront: Voice of Freedom?*

A: That was a good experience, I really enjoyed it. I'm proud of the book, too. Watch this space, there may be more *Homefront* coming in the future. In short, John came up with the idea for the videogame and helped create its universe with the game developers. I came in afterwards and wrote the novel.

Q: How did the character of Spike Berenger of the *Spike Berenger Rock 'n' Roll Hit* series come to be?

A: I'm a huge music fan (and a musician too) and thought it would be fun to write thrillers/mysteries in that world. There's a lot of humor in the books, references to rock music, cameos by rock stars......they were fun to write.

Q: You've written novels based on the video game *Metal Gear*. How did that come to be?

A: With most media tie-in work, a writer is approached by the publisher. The publisher and the videogame company (or movie or TV company, depending on what the property is) make a deal together to do a book. Then the publisher finds the author. Based on my previous work, the publisher hired me to write the two *Metal Gear* books, with Konami's approval.

Q: I was a roleplaying game addict in the 80s, and that extended to the James Bond RPG. What inspired your gaming module *You Only Live Twice II?*

A: I was asked by Victory Games to do one, as I was also a fan of the RPG. I believe they gave me the title–*YOLT II*–and I had to work from that. I tied it into the first *YOLT* game with a few bits in Japan, but then took it off to other original places, like Australia.

Q: What was the process for similar games involving *A View To A Kill* and Stephen King's *The Mist?*

A: That was such a long time ago! My literary agent at the time got me involved with a game developer who was doing those titles. I was into the text adventure games like *Zork* and was very familiar with them. So I was a natural to be hired, especially for the Bond game. I also did *Goldfinger* for the same company.

Q: You wrote the *Pocket Essential Guide to Jethro Tull*. What is the draw for you to their music?

A: I've been a fan since the beginning, or close to it, as their third album was my first. I grew up in a time when progressive rock was popular, and Tull's music spoke to me in ways that others didn't. I've always been a fan. Then, much later, when I learned that Ian Anderson was a Bond fan, I contacted him, sent him some copies of my Bond novels, and we became friends. After that, I wrote the book.

Q: You had two novels were published as e-books in 2011: *Torment*, a supernatural thriller, and *Artifact of Evil*, a thriller using elements of modern day crime, historical characters, and fantasy. What led to the decision to publish them as e-books, and would readers more familiar with your mystery novels see any change in the dynamics of your writing out of what may be considered out of your usual genre?

A: I think so, although I wouldn't say they're out of the usual genre. They're both thrillers. I wrote both novels in 2006 and my agent spent two years trying to sell them to traditional publishers, but as every author in the field knows, not every book gets sold and it's becoming more and more difficult to gets books published. That's why every author I know is now e-publishing backlist titles to which they own the rights as well as never-before-published works that for some reason never sold. I happen to think that *Torment* and *Artifact of Evil* are among my very best books.

Q: *The Black Stiletto* is the story of a female vigilante in the Eisenhower/Kennedy eras, what made you pick the era and the female protagonist?

A: That era is hot now! The whole 50s and 60s time period is being explored a lot more now (a la *"Mad Men*). I'm very proud of this book. It's the first of a series. The second book comes out in May 2012.

Q: Your material is published at a good rate for fans of the genre, so I have to ask, what's in the future for you?

A: Certainly more *Black Stiletto!* I'll also continue writing tie-in novelizations to games and movies. I suggest that fans subscribe to my newsletter through my website www.raymondbenson.com and follow me on Facebook and Twitter for all the latest news.

WESTON OCHSE

Anyone who names his Great Danes Pester, Ghost, Palm Eater, and Goblin Monster Dog is already aces in my book, but when you add the punch of winning the Stoker for Best First Novel for his *Scarecrow Gods*. He's also been known as the Gross Out Contest bouncer. Combine that with the fact he is a practitioner of several martial arts and he's married to a genre author, Yvonne Navarro, and you have a pretty interesting subject for an interview!

Weston can be found online at: WestonOchse.com

Q: In my first interview collection, I interviewed your wife, Yvonne Navarro. What's it like living with another Horror author?

A: Terrific, really. I think it's a pretty rare thing and I'm so glad I'm married to someone who likes what I live, does what I do, and works the craft like I work. We're always talking. We're always communicating. We bounce ideas off each other and commiserate about projects in a way that a non-writer would never understand.

Q: Has there been any talk of you writing a book together?

A: We just did. Yvonne and I wrote the Y.A. novel *Ghost Heart*, coming this summer from Dark Regions Press. It's the story of a teenage boy and girl who travel into the Black Hills and Badlands of South Dakota, each in search of something dear to them.

Q: How did your latest work, *Blood Ocean*, come about?

A: This is a long story, but here it is: I don't know where I was at the time, but I do remember that I heard about a new publishing house called Abaddon Books and asked for their bible about *Afterblight*. I sent a quick pitch, and I mean quick, and I got back an email from Jon Oliver, then Editor-in-Chief of Abaddon, now Editor-in-Chief of both Abaddon and Solaris, that he was intrigued about the idea and would I send him a full pitch, which has a sample chapter as well as a chapter by chapter outline. So I found myself working on this for about a month. In fact, I finished the pitch while I was in a hotel room in Alexandria, Virginia, working on my laptop while the Steelers beat the Colts in the Super Bowl.

My pitch at that time was about Native Americans in the Southwest, who must team up with an L.A. gang of biker samurai to fight off the *Radiant Dawn*—the white folks who want their blood. It was a damn good pitch. I sooo wanted to write that book. But the problem was that every Tom, Dick and English Harry submitted a pitch about Native Americans too.

Needless to say they didn't need me.

So I did what every other writer would do in my shoes……I sulked and wrote something else.

Then about a year later, I was at Book Expo America in Los Angeles. My agent and I went around and had some table-side chats with a few of the editors, one being Jon. This was our first face to face. Being an outgoing person—those of you who know me will agree with this—I enjoy face to face conversations. I thrive on them. Jon and I got to talking. He mentioned that he liked my pitch and was sorry to have to pass on it, but why not send him a pitch for a zombie novel.

A zombie novel? It had never occurred to me to write a zombie novel.

But I did. I sent him a pitch and it became Empire of Salt which sold out everywhere and was a smash hit!

But I still wanted to write an *Afterblight* novel. There'd been a burning inside of me that had not gone away. So even as *Empire of Salt* was premiering in Brighton, England at the World Horror Convention, I was verbally pitching Jon a sprinkle of an idea. He told me to put it on paper when I returned to America and send it to him. I think he saw how eager I was, plus, I think I was keeping him from the pub. So whether or not he meant it or not, I took that as a YES, mentally pumped one arm, and began to work on an idea which revolved around an idea of a monkey being surgically attached to a person's back.

And when I returned to America, I wrote the pitch. It took me about a month as everything came together. And to be totally honest, at first he wasn't sure and didn't accept it right away. But like a dog with a dead rabbit, I shook that idea and shook it, and tweaked the pitch until finally he liked it enough to say those magical five magic words—I'll send you a contract.

Q: *Velvet Dogma* has been called Phillip K. Dick meets William Gibson. Do you feel that's an accurate statement?

A: Yeah. That's a pretty lofty comparison. I forget who made it, but it fits really well. PK Dick was truly groundbreaking in his ability to forecast social issues and wrap them within the framework of a science fiction story. Additionally, William Gibson is the godfather of cyberpunk, a subgenre of science fiction that I hold dear to my heart. Some hardcore science fiction readers see cyberpunk as the gutter, but I've always embraced it's guerilla-like message. Gibson and Stephenson are the demigods of my Cyberpunk Sci Fi Pantheon and it was my distinct pleasure to write within their strata.

Here's the synopsis: In the year 2040, the world has finally achieved the perfect merging of human and machine by developing a method by which the computer has direct integration into the brain. Called Personal Ocular Devices, or PODS, the interface fits over the eye feeding information directly along the optic nerve into the brain, allowing minds and computers to become one.

But not for Rebecca Mines, who has been held in solitary confinement for the last 20 years. Arrested under the 2002 Patriot Act as a cyber-terrorist for unleashing a program called Velvet Dogma, her parole restricts access to all computers and all but the simplest of machines. Although the government is still fearful that she'll resume her previous profession, Rebecca wants nothing more than to find a place to exist in peace. She has a life to live, and twenty years of personal stagnation from which to recover.

But she discovers that things have changed dramatically since she's been in prison. Not only is organ theft sanctioned, but all of her organs have already been levied to the highest bidder. No sooner does she promise the judge that she'll be a law-abiding citizen, then she finds herself on the run from not only Chinese Black Hearts, eager to confiscate her organs, but the authorities who realize that they've let her out too soon.

Q: You've said you never set out to be a Horror writer. Your body of works shows your command of other genres, but what sort of writer had you originally set out to be? Do you think you've reached it?

A: I want to be a full time writer. I want to be able to write, support myself and my wife, live a pretty good life, and travel. I'm not going to slow down until I achieve that. I imagine even if I'm able to achieve it, I probably won't slow down even then.

Q: Can you tell us anything about your upcoming novel from St. Martin's Press, *SEAL Team 666?*

A: Absolutely! It's a novel about a special SEAL Team whose mission it is to protect America from supernatural attack. Within the book is a loose history of this unit which has been known by different names since before the American Revolution. In the novel, you follow the adventure of a young Navy SEAL who is jerked out of BUD/S training and selected for SEAL Team 666 because of several important factors.

Peter Straub is one of my all-time favorite authors. He read it and just loved it. Here's what he said: "Weston Ochse has always been a wised-up, clued-in, completely trustworthy writer of high-action fiction that deserved a wider audience, and *SEAL TEAM 666* is his breakthrough book. Here, every story-line is as taut as a gunfighter's nerves, and individual scenes pop like firecrackers. I raced through this novel and when it ended, I wanted more."

Q: Who would you consider your contemporaries?

A: I guess it depends on how you define contemporaries. There's a whole bunch of us who started writing about the same time. We had the same hopes and dreams. The same drive. The same sort of skewed vision of the universe. We met on HorrorNet in a chat room back in 2007. We'd chat about writing and writers, while folks like Dick Laymon, Ed Lee, Ray Garton, F. Paul Wilson and Tom Piccirilli would come by and bestow upon us great wisdom (in all seriousness). We called ourselves the Cabal. We've achieved varying degrees of success. Which is okay because I think as we grow our definitions of success change as we change. Members of the cabal include Brian Keene, Regina (Garza) Mitchell, Mike Hyuck, Mike Oliveri, Feo Amante, Rain Graves, John Urbancik and Tim Lebbon. We have a bond that still holds strong to this day.

Q: Vampires have long been the most popular creature that readers as well as writers gravitate to, but zombies seem to be on the rise, if you'll pardon the pun. What do you think will be the next creature?

A: Ahh. You want to know the secret. As a member of the Successful Authors Union, I was given this information in a ceremony that involved incense, chanting and naked dancing. Sorry, I can't tell you without the secret high sign.

In all seriousness, I don't think zombies are going anywhere fast (no pun intended). See, the zombie is unlike every other monster in a very specific way. When you write about werewolves, you write about the wolf and how the human fights against the change or embraces it. When you write about vampires, even the sparkly type, you write about the vampire either wanting to suck someone's blood or fighting against it. Both sorts of novels are about the monster. A zombie novel, with very few exceptions, is about people's reaction to a monster. A vampire novel is a monster book and a zombie novel is a people book. Get it?

Q: If you had six months to live, how would you spend them?

A: I'd live my life like I was Kid Rock channeling Ernest Hemingway with the style of Elvis Presley.

Q: Do you have a "Stranded on a deserted island" book you'd have with you?

There's a book on my shelf that I've always wanted to read. It's big. It's thick. It's seminal. But it's also daunting. It's *Dalghren* by Samuel R Delaney.

Q: What's next for you?

A: I have several novellas and short stories due. This summer I'm going to be working on a new novel, but I don't want to talk about it until it's done. Meanwhile, I'm going to be promoting *Blood Ocean* and *SEAL Team 666*, hopefully coming to a bookstore or convention near you.

JACK KETCHUM

Jack knows that things in the dark move slow but sure. He knows their names and that they are disturbingly more human than we'd care to admit. Jack brings them out to fuck with whichever head is trying to wrap itself around his work such as his debut, *Off Season*, and *The Box* which won the Stoker for best short story in 1994 and also received an endorsement from Stephen King saying Jack was the scariest guy in America. Between that an impressive body of novels and short stories, he had also been elected as Grand Master for the 2011 World Horror Convention.

Jack can be found online at: jackketcham.net

Q: *The Girl Next Door* deals with the disturbing theme of child abuse. What made you want to write on that particular slippery slope?

A: People who do this kind of thing royally piss me off. I like to write pissed off. And the sheer scope of the particular crime this was based on—an adult inviting the neighborhood kids in to participate—invited some important themes to explore I think. Herd mentality, corruption of the innocent, secrets, love and regret, heroism and cowardice. Juicy stuff for a writer.

Q: When you wrote the screenplay for *Offspring*, did you come across any problems unique to the mechanics of the screenplay? There's the Hollywood cliché, but true, saying that when adapting a screenplay, the first thing you do is throw out the source material?

A: Oh yeah, I was about to throw out my own source material. Sure. One of the things that make the films based on my books unusual is the attention the various writers and directors have given to staying as close as possible to the source material. I wasn't about to do otherwise. The major change from book to movie was letting The Woman live at the end, but that wasn't in my screenplay. My screenplay killed her. But director Andrew Van den Houten saw how good Pollyanna McIntosh was in the part and said no, she's gotta live, she needs another movie. And I'm glad he did.

Q: There have been two *Offspring* movies thus far. Is this the beginning of a franchise?
A: I hate that word. It brings to mind greasy hamburgers. Lucky McKee and I have talked about doing a sequel to *The Woman* at some point, but we agree that the themes and subject matter have to be as unique and unusual as that film. No Jasons or Freddies, please.

Q: With being called "The Scariest Man In America" by Stephen King, does that effect your mindset when you sit down to wrote?
A: Not at all. I don't always set out to be scary. Fiction's all about character and story. Some of my stuff's not scary at all, though I'll admit to an inclination in that direction. I'm happy as all hell that Steve said it, though. That comment's still selling books for me.

Q: You handle some of the disturbing or disgusting traits of the human condition, sometimes questioning in *The Woman* that monsters can be the anybody, not just the disfigured serial killer. What motivated you and/or continues to motivate you to turn that particular stone over?

I think I just like reminding people that there are monsters everywhere. You don't have to be a serial killer to be a sociopath, to be minus the empathy gene. You can be a son with his mother strapped to a bed so that he can cash her social security checks. You can be the inventor of a ponzi scheme. You can be a kid posting vicious hate-mail on the internet. So neighbor, girlfriend, business associate, whatever—buyer beware. Always.

Q: What benchmark, if any, do you use to avoid the explicit from becoming the exploitive?
A: No benchmark really except my own intuition. I often use a very flat line for the violent stuff, so that it's not all gussied up with adjectives and adverbs. Which, when misused, can be kinda salacious.

Q: *The Girl Next Door* continues to haunt me. As it was based upon a true story, how did you first learn about it, and what changes were made to fit your vision of a fictional story?

I came upon Gertie and Sylvia first in J. Robert Nash's *Bloodletters And Badmen* and was struck, not only by the crime, but by the photo of Gert. She haunted me, and I knew I wanted to write about her. But the crime took place in Indiana and I don't know a thing about

Indiana. Then my mother died and I'd go back and forth from New York to New Jersey for a few months to settle her affairs and get used to losing both her and the home I grew up in. And at some point I realized I could set the story there, on that dead-end street back in the 50s and early 60s. I whittled down the real family to just three boys and posited a boy next door who is witness to the proceedings, pondered how he'd feel about his participation as a grown-up, and told the story from that point of view.

Q: What was the inspiration behind *Right to Life?*
A: I read about these idiots who kidnapped a woman in order to bring her to term. Then, a block away from me, we had a clinic over a bank and there were these right-to-lifers picketing every day. I still have one of the little pink plastic fetuses they were handing out in a tray above my desk. The bank eventually refused to renew the clinic's lease. Did I mention that I write a lot from anger?

Q: And, as clichéd as a question this is, I have to ask the scariest guy in America, what scares you?
A: First, Alzheimer's. Second, snakes. You can read all about the latter in my story of the same name in *Peaceable Kingdom*.

Q: How would you like your tombstone to read?

A: I sorta want my ashes scattered to the wind. But I guess HE HAD A DAMN GOOD TIME would do.

RAYMOND FEIST

Raymond is no stranger to the successes Speculative Fiction can bring to a determined author. He has been on the New York Times Best-Seller List, thanks to his superlative books such as *Magician*, *Silverthorn*, and *A Darkness at Sethanon*, which complete The Riftwar Saga, the first series in the Arc that has since become known as the Riftwar Cycle. Following this, he penned *The Serpentwar Saga*, and *The Riftwar Legacy* series which is based in part, on the hugely successful computer games set in his universe, *Betrayal at Kondor and Return to Kondor* which are the basis for the computer games of the same name.

Raymond can be found online at: http://www.crydee.com/

Q: Who are your contemporaries?

A: Contemporaries? I guess that depends on how you define it. If you mean "people published the same time I am," we can start with Homer and end with whoever has a first fantasy novel published this week. If you mean people who broke in more or less about the same time I did, that list is out there for anyone who wants to look at publishing since 1982. There are some obvious names, Robert Jordan, Joel Rosenberg, George R.R. Martin, etc.

Q: Did the authors you read as a child influence you as much as those you read as you grew older?

A: Childhood authors influence you more, I think, as they tend to set the paradigm of what you love more than what you admire for craft or being clever or any other less visceral reaction. I grew up on "Boys Adventure Fiction," of the late 19th early 20th Century and historical novels, and that influenced me far more than the fantasy I read in college.

Q: With your experience as an author, is it difficult for you to read stories just for the pleasure of being the reader?

A: I read for fun. I just don't read fantasy. I read history, biography, politics, spy thrillers, action/adventure.

Q: I know you're an admirer of Shakespeare. Out of curiosity, what do you think of films like *Shakespeare in Love* and more recently, *Anonymous*?

A: Haven't seen *Anonymous*, but *Shakespeare in Love* was charming. It worked on several levels, and one of the best was showing non-writers how often writers grind what's around them into the details of story.

Q: What's your opinion regarding e-books? It seems to be the next step in self publishing as well as for those who could be found of the New York Time's Best Seller List?

A: E-books are here, and they will grow. So, I really don't have an opinion on them. We still don't have a good idea of how they fit into the ecology of the publishing market, but that will come into focus soon. As for the NYTs, they're pretty conservative, so by the time they have a list of ebooks, you'll know they've arrived finally.

Q: One of my favorite books of yours is *Faerie Tale*. What went into your building that world?

A: *Faerie Tale* was a challenge, because I took some diverse premises and wove them together into an improbable cloth. The setting was mundane, but the magic was merely a glimpse away. Holding that perspective from start to finish was the hard part. Kids talking baseball one page, then the thing under the bed the next, that was some of the hardest stuff to write I've ever done.

Q: What was it like working with Janny Wurts for the Empire Series?

A: Janny and I argued a lot, but we always found a better solution for that. She was a great experience as a writing partner, as I learned how to look at things with different eyes. She has an artist's sensibilities and is very visual. I really am happy with how our series turned out.

Q: You once mentioned having wanted to write an "Elmore Leonard" type book, and a Western. Have either of these become closer to becoming a reality?

A: My non-fantasy projects always seem to get pushed back. Maybe if I win the Lotto I can just write what I want, but for the near future, more fantasy.

Q: What was the inspiration behind the Demonwar Saga?

A: *Demonwar* was based on the concept of a route army, but on a dimensional scale. You beat the hell out of the other guys army, and instead of surrendering, they take off. Once that happens, they're not beat anymore, but seriously dangerous like rats clawing their way out of a corner. It was a nice thing to slug into the longer narrative because it's not what it looks like at first glance. In fact, the truth about the *Demonwar* doesn't come out until this very last book I'm writing in the ChaosWar Saga.

Q: What can we expect from *A Crown Imperiled*?

A: *Crown Imperiled* is the 2nd act of a 3-act play, so you'll see bridging action, new sets of problems revealed, and hopefully have fun reading it.

Q: Are there any new clichés in the Fantasy genre?

A: By its nature, there can't be "new" clichés. They have to be around a while and get used a lot before they're clichés. There may be new trends that will become that, but as I don't read other people's fantasy, I can't tell you what they are.

Q: Which new authors, if any, do you enjoy reading?

A: Don't read new authors. My reading time is so scant someone needs to hang around awhile before I get to them.

Q: You've created several worlds in a variety of series. Have there been any particular challenges in creating each world as richly unique as you have?

A: The challenge to world building is to make it "make sense," i.e. each planet has to have an ecology that seems to make sense to the reader, even if an ecologist is doubled up laughing.

Q: What is on the horizon for you, as a person as well as an author?

A: As a person, seeing my kids off to college (one there already, the other a year away), putting a little by for old age (too late, probably), having as much fun as I can squeeze out of a day, and keep writing until I grow bored with it. For the future, I'll do a non-Midkemian series next, which looks to be a three book package, about which I'll say no more.

SCOTT LEBERECHT, EDUARDO SANCHEZ, and MATT COMPTON

With the constant "spectacle above substance" approach constantly shoved towards the average moviegoer, complete with stunt casting, a committee of suits who think they're writers, and more Surprise rather than Scary Factor, it's refreshing when small-budget films like *The Blair Witch Project* or *Paranormal Activity* get the attention they deserve. They hearken back to a time when horror meant thrills, creepiness, and God forbid, a story that produces characters unique and true to themselves.

Thus, Writer/Director Scott Leberecht conceived *Midnight Son*, and through the collaboration and help of Producer Matt Compton and some guy named Eduardo Sanchez (Executive Producer) who co-created *The Blair Witch Project*, they were able to give us, the viewer, a small budget horror film that has its head tilted just a little off to the side…

Q: The cinematic representation of claustrophobic isolation is especially dynamic. Was that an intentional aspect of the cinematography?

SL: Feeling the walls closing in on Jacob was something Lyn Moncrief (Director of Photography) and I definitely wanted to achieve. We selected framing that creates a claustrophobic effect, but we also chose locations that were going to box us in and naturally limit our options. I would say most of it was intentional, but there were definitely times we had no choice.

ES: This was definitely one of the aspects that originally drew me into this film after I saw some raw footage of what Scott and Lyn had shot. They were smart with their angles and locations choices, showing us just enough to make the world work but not over-reaching, which is what a lot of really low budget films do, mostly to their detriment.

Q: What prompted the specific use of the *Fright Night* clip as Jacob researches what vampires are?

SL: I am a sick fan of that film, and I think I watched it a hundred times as a kid. When I was writing the bit where Jacob researches and tests his "vampirism," I thought of the scene where Evil Ed is burned by the crucifix. There are a lot of vampire films that have this moment, but *Fright Night* felt best for us. There is a campy, funny quality to it that contrasted with, and gave some relief to, the heavy tone of *Midnight Son*. There was talk of casting a couple actors and shooting a similar scene, which would have been cheaper than securing rights, but ultimately I felt he needed to watch a real vampire film—something that exists in our world, to ground it in a reality the audience could relate to.

ED: This was one of the first things we told Scott that we'd have to cut out when Matt and I first came on board. There was no way we were going to be able to afford this clip from *Fright Night*. But Scott insisted, found out that the numbers weren't that crazy and we ended up keeping the clip, which in the end, really adds a lot to the film. It's Scott's tip of the hat to a solid classic.

Q: What led to the decision to have vampirism as a disease in the movie?

SL: Truth is, I never really set out to make a vampire movie. It just became the perfect vehicle for a story I wanted to tell about a young man coping with his transformation into something he believes is 'wrong' or 'evil'. Treating it as a congenital illness—rather than an infection by some outside organism—played into the idea of my character being antagonized by his own body. Events like puberty, sexual attraction, and falling in love are all things that happen to us from the inside out. We generally dislike being at the mercy of anything, but when the thing we don't want emanates from within, our self-image shatters. We must cope with a new set of rules, and our identity is temporarily on hold. These are very scary moments in life, and it is always what I wanted to explore.

ED: It's what I really love about the film and why I was so intrigued when I first read the script. There's never the obligatory "fun being a vampire" section that most vampire stories have. In fact, the only character that seems to relish it is the main bad guy in the film, and that kind of morality was what I liked in the script and now in the film. It's a disease, and that's why we really feel for Jacob. It's the glue that holds the story together.

Q: The chemistry between Zak Kilberg and Maya Parish is remarkable from their first meeting onscreen. How did you find these two?

SL: I saw Maya Parish in a short film directed by a colleague while attending the American Film Institute in Los Angeles. At the time, I was writing *Midnight Son*, and thought she could be right for the role of Mary. I approached her after the screening, and said I may have a part for her. Years later, I sent her the script. She loved it and agreed to play the part. Zak Kilberg was led to a website I created early on to raise awareness and support as I we neared production. He sent me a headshot and I thought he looked perfect for the lead role. I was living in San Francisco at the time, and he was in LA. He then shot a video, acting in a scene I had written. I loved it, and wanted to meet him. After that meeting, I knew he was right for the role and didn't bother to audition anyone else. As far as their chemistry goes, I like to think there was some weird metaphysical harmony at work.

Q: Matt, Ed, how did you discover Scott's work?
MC: Ed approached me about it. He had read the script and seen a little bit of footage, and liked both. He asked me if I'd be interested in coming on as Producer, while we would be an Executive Producer (along with friend & colleague Reed Frerichs).

I read the script, and thought it was quite original. I had never seen a vampire story told that way before. Ed, Scott and I met for lunch one day in LA, and he showed us some of the dailies. The cinematography looked really good, and the acting was great. I felt like he had something special here, and I wanted to be a part of it. Almost three years later, here we are with a finished movie. It's feels great to finally be able to show it to audiences after so much work!

ES: I was mixing Seventh Moon at Skywalker Sound and one of the sound editors, David Hughes, approached me about this cool film he was working on, *Midnight Son*. He thought it was really special, so he got Scott and me hooked up. I read the script, saw the footage and was sold.

That's when I contacted Matt Compton and Reed Frerichs to see if they wanted to help and they were impressed with it just like I was. Matt came on as a full producer and Reed and I became executive producers and the rest is history.

Q: The soundtrack is spacious. What led to the decision to take that approach?

SL: Kays Alatrakchi is a brilliant musician. This was our first time working together, and I learned a lot from him. His instinct to keep the music spacious turned out to be exactly the right approach. In order to achieve realism, we shot using a somewhat documentary style, so the score had to exist in a space between the lines—on an almost unconscious level—but it also had to be powerful enough to elicit an emotional reaction. The ability to create music that stands alone, supports a narrative, and somehow does not call attention to itself is big challenge. Kays is one of the hardest working artists I've met in a long time. He embraced this challenge with a truckload of ideas and the courage to walk that tightrope.

ES: Kays is someone Matt and I knew from back in the day in Orlando. He's a great guy and a very talented composer. I think he hit a home run with this score, probably my favorite of his work. Like Scott said, it's just the right mixture of subtlety and power.

Q: Scott, Your appreciation for David Lynch is obvious in *Midnight Son*. Do you have a favorite film of his?

SL: I do appreciate Lynch. I would say my favorite movie of his is *Blue Velvet*.

Q: Judging by his apartment, Jacob's a reader…what's on his shelf and why?

SL: I imagine Jacob reads a lot of fantasy, adventure and science fiction—Jules Verne, Edgar Rice Burroughs, Ray Bradbury, Terry Brooks—anything to escape his lonely, sedentary life. I also imagine he has a lot of pornographic magazines and adult comic books. His favorite would probably be *Ripple* by Dave Cooper.

Q: How did you choose which things could or couldn't harm someone in Jacob's condition? For instance, a cross won't, but sunlight is fatal. They do not have superhuman strength, but their will to live is…well, paranormal.

SL: I don't think Jacob's will to live is paranormal. He just has to do what he must to survive. He is very mortal, and has been thrown a new set of rules to cope with, as a mortal. Writing draft after draft of the screenplay made me realize that anything that made it cool to be a vampire had to go. I kept the blood and sunlight problems because those are the two things I personally would hate to deal with on a daily basis. I believe my unconscious goal was to make the audience feel like they've been lied to all these years, and that being a vampire would, in reality, suck.

ES: Like I said earlier, in MS, vampirism is a disease, a sickness that has to be dealt with like any other attack on the body. It was a great choice that Scott made during the process, a completely realistic and unglamorous look at this condition. And besides his thirst for blood and the healing ability, he's just a normal dude trying to deal with the shitty hand that life has dealt him.

I always wonder what other abilities Jacob has that he hasn't discovered yet. Could be a very cool sequel.

Q: Ed, how has being the Co-Creator of *Blair* changed your view and vision of horror in cinema?

ES: Well, it's completely shaped it, really. I wasn't much of a horror person until we did *BW*. I mean, I liked horror films, but I didn't give it any special attention. Now, I have to keep my finger on the pulse of what is out there. And because of *BW*, I feel like I'm a part of this eclectic family. The fans are so amazing and so dedicated to this genre. It never ceases to surprise me. I feel privileged to be a small part of it.

Q: There are rumblings of another *Blair* film. What can you tell us?

ES: We are as close as we've ever been to making another *Blair* film a reality, but I really can't say more. And even that doesn't guarantee that another *Blair* film will be made. It's still very much up in the air. We are making progress, though.

JOE SCHREIBER

Joe's blog is called The Scary Parent, and has written in the Expanded *Star Wars* Universe with *Red Harvest*, and the *Dawn of the Dead Meets Star Wars, Death Troopers,* considered the first combination of SF and H for that franchise. Throw in his superlative work such as *Chasing the Dead* and *Au Revoir, Crazy European Chick*. For some reason, I felt a connection to Joe's view on being a writer of things dark as well as a parent.

Joe's spots in cyberspace are http://scaryparent.blogspot.com/ and http://joeschreiber.blogspot.com/

Q: What's the average day for someone referred to as 'The Scary Parent?'

A: I get up with my kids at 7:00 a.m.. Hang out with them for a couple hours—they're homeschooled, so I do a bit of that with them—then if there's nothing else going on, start writing around nine. Finish around noon, a little more kid time, then head off to the hospital where I work. Get out around eleven at night. Eat cold pizza and watch *The Hangover 2*, then stumble off to bed. Repeat as necessary.

Q: Are your kids fans of *Star Wars*?

A: Not at all. My son's into Super Mario and something called Skylanders. My daughter likes Harry Potter and *Diary of a Wimpy Kid*. They like hanging out with stormtroopers at the book signings, but that's about the extent of it...

Q: How did they react to their father's rather dark take of the *Star Wars* Universe, *Deathtroopers*?

A: They liked the cover, although the posters of it in the basement kind of freak them out. Occasionally they'll ask questions about the story, and they might eventually read it, but I'm not holding my breath. Meanwhile, they draw pictures on the backs of the proof pages that have accumulated around the house.

Q: What can you tell us about the development of what is basically the Horror side of the *Star Wars* literary franchise?

A: It was an amazingly smooth process. I got a call from my editor at the time, at Random House, who asked if I'd consider writing a zombie *Star Wars* novel. I said yes, and started working on an outline. Lucasfilm had some notes, and I went back and rewrote it, then tackled the book. Eight weeks later, the first draft was done. They were incredibly supportive and encouraging throughout the entire process, a dream to work with, really.

Q: Writing in such a beloved universe where fans are at times rabid and unforgiving, did you have any trepidations about taking *Star Wars* into dark territory?

A: Not really. When I sit down to write anything, all the pressure that I feel comes from within. Can I pull it off? Can I actually write a story that's going to hold my interest, and develop it all the way through? All that stress goes away once you fall into the story and find your path but until then, it can be pretty scary. I figured that *Star Wars* fans would either like it, or they wouldn't, but first I needed to make sure I did the best job that I could do.

Q: Red Harvest was another dark *Star Wars* story. Did its development mirror that of *Deathtroopers?* And is the title a play on the *Star Wars* film codename *Blue Harvest?*

A: The title is definitely a play on *Blue Harvest.* I was contracted to write that book before *Death Troopers* was even released, and there was a lot of back and forth on that one, developing the world of the Old Republic. It was fun to be able to use Jedi and Sith in a zombie environment.

Q: Which character or set of characters in the Star Wars Universe would you like to write a novel about? Would it be a horror story?

A: Horror tends to be my default mode, so my guess is that it probably would go that way. My favorite *Star Wars* characters are the ones that we'd recognize from our world, or at least our pop culture universe—the inexperienced farm boy yearning for something bigger, the rogue who lives by his own moral code, the tough princess. Having said that, I love writing about stormtroopers. I think it would be great to do another story about the guys who wear the armor, Vader's Fist, encountering something way beyond their pay grade.

Q: Do you have a favorite *Star Wars* movie?

A: *Empire*, hands down.

Q: Is there any other franchise you'd like to write for?

A: Great question. I'm not sure, honestly—although I think an *Alien* novel would be a lot of fun.

Q: The *Supernatural* novel you did, *The Unholy Cause*, resonated with me because of the Biblical connection and the noose Judas hung himself with. I know you immersed yourself in *Supernatural* continuity, but was there much research into Judas or the noose? Not a whole lot is out there?

A: I'm not exactly the world's greatest researcher. Lazy is probably a generous way of describing it. I'd like to say that I spent hours researching archaic apocryphal texts and ancient books of knots, but that would be a lie. Mostly, I just made it up.

Q: With *No Doors, No Windows*, you established an almost Serlingesque pacing to this very patient, deliberate story. It seemed to me your previous novels were a bit faster paced. Did you approach this novel with that intent?

A: Absolutely. With *No Doors*, I was very much aware that this would be my last horror novel for a while, and I was taking a shot at the haunted house genre, so I was definitely shooting for a slow-burn creep fest a la Shirley Jackson, instead of the balls-out adrenaline blast of horror like the couple before it. I'm guessing the three or four people who read the thing probably agreed.

Q: A favorite novel of yours for me is *Chasing the Dead*. It plays upon some very visceral fears as person and parent. How did you refine such an emotional response without going for the easier aspects that seem to be so prominent in movies and lit?

A: I'm really not sure. *Chasing the Dead* was written from my nerve endings, in the most compulsive and direct way I knew how, and I didn't really have anything to compare it to, let alone emulate, so maybe that's why. It's very much the work of a new parent who was working two jobs and didn't have a lot of extra time to mess around. It's raw, almost a bit ugly in its urgency, but that was how I felt at the time.

Q: How is the development of the *Eat the Dark* and *Chasing the Dead* coming along? The cliché is that when you adapt material for a screenplay, you toss out the source material...

A: I know! I'm adapting *Eat the Dark* myself, and it is quite different from the book. but that's okay—it's kind of the book's twitchier, untrustworthy meth-head brother. But it's a lot of fun. The outlook for *Chasing the Dead* is a bit more nebulous. It's still being developed, and the script I read was quite good, but so much of the process has to do with the guys who handle the money, so we'll see.

Q: Your latest, *Au Revoir, Crazy European Chick* is sort of a sideways *Le Femme Nikita* with a lot of humor and aimed at a Young Adult audience. Will we see a series stem from this? Maybe a movie?

A: There's a sequel due out this fall, set in Europe, and Paramount has the movie rights with Josh Schwartz attached to direct, so we'll see.

Q: What scares the Scary Parent?

A: The Visa bill...

CAITLIN R. KIERNAN

While her fiction had gained notice in previous years, in May 1996, Caitlin was approached by Neil Gaiman and editors at DC/Vertigo Comics to begin writing for *The Dreaming*, a spin-off from Gaiman's groundbreaking *The Sandman*. She wrote the book until its conclusion in 2001. She has consistently eschewed the label of "horror writer" but has certainly placed her own dynamic mark on the fiction of the dark and weird.

You can catch her online at: caitlinrkiernan.com

Q: How does a paleontologist become a SF/DF fiction author?

A: The paleontologist comes to a place in her life where continuing to be a paleontologist ceases to be a viable option, and so she has to turn to an utterly ridiculous Plan B. Luckily, though, the paleontologist is well-read and has some talent as a writer, and people think having been a paleontologist is interesting and so they remember you. But none of this means anything at all unless the former paleontologist is incredibly lucky. Highly unlikely, but weird shit happens all the time. Well, not so much *weird* shit, as shit that is merely highly improbable.

Q: Your first novel, *The Five of Cups*, was written between 1992-1993, but didn't see publication until 2003. What's the story behind the delay?

A: Well, I did try to sell it immediately after it was written. I almost sold it right off, and it *did* get me my first agent. But it's actually a pretty lousy novel. I was only just learning how to construct a novel, and I was lucky enough that every editor who read it rejected it. All those rejections, they led to my agent, that first agent who's no longer my agent, asking me to write another book. One that wasn't about vampires, please. So, I forced myself to step away from "horror," and I wrote *Silk*, which was, instead, published as my first novel. But over the years, readers had an interest in my "lost novel." It was actually called that. Someone at a con actually offered a friend of mine five-hundred dollars if he could get this person a copy. Finally, all those years later, I let it be published, mostly as a curiosity. So people could see how it began, I suppose. But, truthfully, I can't stand to look at the thing. I try not to talk about that book.

Q: You worked very closely with Neil Gaiman on DC Comics/Vertigo's *The Dreaming*, what was it like working with him and getting the chance to play in his universe?

A: Neil is wonderful. He gave me some of my first breaks, including the *Dreaming* gig. And *The Sandman* is brilliant. Unfortunately, by the time I was asked to write for *The Dreaming*—a series that never should have happened to begin with—was already hopelessly broken. There were all these readers who wanted *The Sandman: The Next Generation*. And that's not what they got. So this spin-off limped along for sixty issues, most of which I wrote, a few of which I love, before someone thankfully pulled the plug. By the way, I'd asked to leave the series at the fiftieth issue, and was persuaded to stay on. I was told the series would last a long time. Reluctantly, I agreed. Then it died ten issues later. But. Playing with Neil's characters, many whom I loved and still do, that part was marvelous. It's just that working for DC Vertigo was a nightmare. It paid the bills, probably better than my bills had ever before been paid, but the shiny wore off after my first six or seven issues. Neil knows how I feel about *The Dreaming*. I made the best of a bad situation. In the end, it taught me to be a professional, to handle deadlines and what have you. And, yeah, working with Neil was great. There are even a few bits of actual secret collaboration strewn here and there through the series. Mostly, he'd give me permission to write one of the Endless, and I'd ask him to write that character's dialogue.

Q: *The Drowning Girl: A Memoir* has a very compelling trailer on your website. Can you tell us about the making of it?

A: Well, we're still working on the full one-minute cut, the final. But so far it's been grand. First, it was incredible to see the response from my readers when I set out to crowdsource a book trailer. We set it up on Kickstarter, asking for $1,200, but the donations came to more than three times that. We found our cast and crew, and filmed in Massachusetts and Rhode Island, on location, and almost the whole experience was genuinely wonderful. Sara Murphy, the actor who played Eva, was a trooper. We'd planned to shoot in the summer, but were delayed until the autumn, after the weather turned cold. One scene, which she had to do in the nude on a country road, she did it in a rain so hard we could hardly hear each other over. Then, the next day, we were filming in the Blackstone River Gorge, and the river was freezing. Never mind the current. She was willing to do another nude scene, crawling out of that river. I was standing there expecting to have to go in after her at any moment. Oh, and the first day, Sara walked into three-foot surf at Moonstone Beach. She was amazing. And the footage is wonderful. Nicola Astles, who plays the book's protagonist, Imp, she had the unenviable task of playing out a scene where Imp tries to drown herself, and I fear we almost managed to *actually* drown her in the process.

Q: What can we expect from *The Drowning Girl?*

A: It's not like anything I've ever done. I was terrified I'd spent two years writing something awful, something illegible, unreadable. But then Peter Straub read it and loved it. In fact, he went so far as to say he'd never read anything like it before, and that it was my masterpiece. Still, if people go in expecting a genre horror novel, they're going to be very, very disappointed. It's the memoir of a schizophrenic girl who may, or may not, have met and fallen in love with a ghost, and the ghost may, or may not, be a mermaid. Or a werewolf. There's a wonderful line from a Kelly Link story, "Pretty Monsters"—*Stories shift their shape.* And that line sort of sums up the novel. Just when you think it's this, it becomes that. But if you believe it's that, maybe it's this, after all. What should people expect? A book about schizophrenia, more than anything. But also a book about hauntings, about the nature of hauntings. Which may, or may not, make it a ghost story. But not in the tradition that a lot of people have come to expect. Not a book where I'm necessarily setting out to scare you. Go back to *The Turn of the Screw,* or *Rebecca,* or *Gaslight,* or *The Haunting of Hill House.* This is a story about the human mind, and how it shapes reality, how those perceptions of reality are constantly shifting their shapes.

Q: I know you're not fond of being pegged as a 'horror author,' but *The Red Tree* has a creepy elegance to it. Are you ever aware of *not* being a horror writer when writing a work like that?

A: To quote—or paraphrase—Douglas Winter: "Writing isn't a genre. It's an emotion." I write stories filled with horror, terror, awe, fear, wonder, beauty, sorrow, epiphany, and on and on and on. *The Red Tree*, it might all add up to something that instills a sense of dread. Or whatever. But so does *Apocalypse Now*, and people don't generally claim Coppola was making a horror film. For that matter, sort of looking at this problem from another direction, if I buy into the idea that we have to label people "horror" writers, "science fiction" writers, "fantasy" writers...what the hell do we do with someone like Harlan Ellison? Or Ray Bradbury? Angela Carter? Cormac McCarthy? Kathe Koja? Kurt Vonnegut, Jr.? William Burroughs? Genre is primarily a marketing paradigm, and has very little to do with what any given writer does.

Q: Are there any plans to bring *The Red Tree* to the silver screen? Has there been any interest from filmmakers to adapt your work?
A: There's been a lot of interest, and there still is. It comes and goes. *Threshold* came very close in 2002. When it all fell apart, well, it was hard enough that I learned to forget about Hollywood. If it happens, it happens. If it happens and the resulting movie isn't shit, that would be wonderful, and I'd be happy. I love film. But it's not something I think about when I'm writing or daydreaming. A producer or a director shows interest, and, well, it's not my job to think about those sorts of things. Anyway, if there are any current plans to film *The Red Tree*, no one's told me.

Q: Do you have a favorite work of yours?

A: Definitely *The Drowning Girl*. No question. With *The Red Tree* a close second, and my short-story collections *A is for Alien* and *Confessions of a Five-Chambered Heart*.

Q: The narrative tone of your work has been compared to the likes of H.P. Lovecraft and Algernon Blackwood. Do you feel that's an accurate comparison?

A: Yes and no. I've definitely looked back to Lovecraft, Blackwood, Lord Dunsany, Arthur Machen, Ambrose Bierce, to learn a lot of what I know. The importance of mood, for example. Restraint, for another. But I've never written what could be called pastiche, as some admirers of Lovecraft have done. I'd never do such a thing. Not even if I'm using elements from his fiction. But, too, there are a lot of influences I think have been overlooked recently, because some people want to peg me as one of the new flag bearers of the weird or whatever. The Modernists are a huge influence, especially Faulkner. A lot of poets, more than I could name. Angela Carter and Shirley Jackson have been huge influences, as have Harlan Ellison and Peter Straub. But I could go on like this for hours.

Q: Is it fair to say that *Silk* was the book that put you on the map, so to speak?

A: I think it's completely fair. It was my first published novel, and it may not have been a bestseller, but it wasn't unsuccessful. I think it led a lot of other authors to expect a lot from me in the future, which was, at the time, terrifying. Honestly, I don't think I lived up to that potential until *The Red Tree*.

Q: As a paleontologist, you have many fossils in your home. Do you have a particular favorite?

A: You know, I've got cabinets filled with beautiful trilobites and ammonites from all around the world, with dinosaur and mosasaur bones and fossil turtles. But, if I had to pick a personal favorite, it's a tiny squashed trilobite, may five mm. long, on a chunk of shale. I collected it when I was thirteen, and when I showed it to paleontologists at a museum in Birmingham, they were very excited about it and asked me to lead them to the road cut where I'd found it. Which led to my volunteering at the museum. Which led to my working at the museum… and so forth. So much happened because that one tiny trilobite.

Q: What does a typical day entail for you?

A: If I'm lucky, I'm out of bed by ten-thirty or eleven. I'm a night person. So, I have breakfast and coffee. I read email. I write a LiveJournal entry. Then I answer all that email I read earlier. Then I write. I go weeks at a time without leaving the house. I just repeat this day-to-day cycle. I don't know how I haven't died of monotony. I meet people who see being an author as a glamorous life. And I want to say, you ought to see me sitting at my desk in my underwear—I usually write in a tank top and underwear—and watch me sitting there typing, day after day after day. It's about as glamorous as watching grass grow.

Q: Given an hour over coffee (or beverage of your choice) with anyone alive or dead, who would it be, and what topics would you like to talk about?

A: I have no idea. Maybe David Bowie, in which case we'd talk about sex and music, Outsider art and what it's like to kiss Catherine Deneuve.

Q: You've called collections like your *Confessions of a Five-Chambered Heart* "Weird erotica." How is your "Weird erotica" defined?

A: There are things that defy definition. Or that it's just too much trouble to define. I call it "weird erotica" because I figured people would want me to call it something. Angela Carter and the Marquis de Sade get together and write a story about a drug-fueled gay masked ball that culminates with a performance of Oscar Wilde's *Salomé* wherein the title role is played by a nude pre-op transsexual. Or, H.P. Lovecraft and Anaïs Nin and Bill Burroughs get together and write a story about a cannibal and her willing victim, who's also her lover, who's being consumed over months and months, and who takes part in the feasts of her flesh. That's "weird erotica."

Q: What can you tell your readers about yourself that they probably don't know?

A: I was a born with a tail. Unfortunately, most of it was removed at birth. All that's left visible is a tiny little nub of cartilage.

WILLIAM NOLAN

While he is best known for coauthoring the novel *Logan's Run* with George Clayton Johnson, he also co-wrote the screenplay for the 1976 horror film *Burnt Offerings* which starred Karen Black and Bette Davis. His nonfiction books are of such ambitious studies of a variety of fields and genres *John Huston: King Rebel, Carnival of Speed, The Ray Bradbury Companion, Dashiell Hammett: A Casebook* and numerous others. In 2010, he received the Lifetime Achievement Stoker award from the Horror Writers Association. It was my honor to interview a man whose work I grew up reading.

williamfnolan.com is the place to find him online.

Q: I guess I'll start by asking a popular question of late; What's going on with the remake of *Logan's Run*?

A: "They" (the Hollywood trade papers) say that the new version will be produced this year... I'll believe it when it happens (after fifteen years of waiting!). All fingers crossed...

Q: What did you think of the radio production of *Logan's Run* in 2011?

A: I thought it was well-produced.

Q: What was in the decision making of having Paul Salamoff write *Logan's Run: Aftermath*?

A: That was decided by the publisher (Bluewater Productions). Jason V Brock and I acted as Costume Designers and Story Consultants. Actually, the "Future History" section of the first series is all by Jason—even the parts in the comic are his writing, verbatim!

Q: Did you initially imagine the *Logan* saga to be the trilogy of *Logan's Run, Logan's World*, and *Logan's Search*?

A: No. I also went on to write *Logan's Return* (a novelette) and am completing another new part of the series, *Logan's Journey* (with Paul McComas). Jason and I are also gearing up to do a major retake on *Logan* as well: *Logan Falls*.

Q: Having written *Logan's Run* with George Clayton Johnson, I was wondering if the two of you still keep in touch?

A: Oh, sure. We see each other at least once a year. We're still good friends!

Q: You've written other works, does it ever get to you that *Logan's Run* looms over anything else?

A: Not at all! I'm grateful to have Logan as my "calling card." It's one of the high points of my 60-year career! I'm proud to be "Logan's Papa."

Q: You wrote a film treatment for John W. Campbell's story "Who Goes There?". Having done that, what's your take on the films that ended up being made from Campbell's source novella, such as Howard Hawks' *The Thing From Another World* in 1951, John Carpenter's *The Thing* in 1982, and the 2011 version?

A: I didn't see the most recent version, but I liked both of the other versions. That said, I think that my version would have made a better picture.

Q: What was it like working with *Dark Shadows* creator Dan Curtis for the film *Burnt Offerings*?

A: Dan and I were pals...I worked on seventeen projects with him. We got along fine, and he had great respect for my work. Interestingly, *Burnt Offerings* at the time was just another of our many projects together, but now has a life of its own. I'm proud of it.

Q: *The Seven For Space* series features a classic sort of gumshoe in a futuristic setting. What inspired that?

A: I've always loved wild humor. (I discovered S. J. Perelman in high school—and I also love James Thurber.) One of my closest friends is the comedian Stan Freberg, who's a *very* funny guy!

Q: *Seven For Space* was not only Science Fiction, but also humorous without being mean-spirited towards the genre. Who influences your sense of humor?

A: Everyone and everything... I find humor everywhere. I read Sheckley and Goulart in SF, and they influenced the *Space* series.

Q: What went into writing *How to Write Horror Fiction*?

A: I was teaching creative writing at a college and was asked about horror fiction in particular as a genre. (Another book I did that is worthwhile is the more general writing primer called *Let's Get Creative!*)

Q: Have you ever been concerned that you may be pigeonholed as only an SF writer?

A: Sometimes. I mean, I've done SF, true, but also fantasy, horror, biography, poetry, crime, comics, and a wide variety of short fiction… And only a handful of those are SF. The label doesn't really fit me; no one label does!

Q: What attracted you to the works of Dashiell Hammett?

A: I read Chandler first, and I loved his stuff. A friend said to me: "If you like Chandler, you'll dig Hammett." Of course, he was right! I love 'em both: Hard, tough, but poetic. They're the best, I feel.

Q: You're self-confessed movie fanatic. What films have you seen recently that you were really affected by?

A: I thought that *War Horse* was lovely. *The Grey* was a marvelous wilderness picture…I try to see a new movie each week. (Since age five!) Films have been a huge influence in my life.

Q: Is there a book that you wish you've written?

A: No, or I would have!

Q: You knew James Dean. What can you tell us about your relationship with him?

A: I knew Dean only slightly. We met at the road races in California. He was a very fast driver, but he pushed too hard. His death in a car crash didn't surprise me.

Q: Anything you'd like to say to your fans to sign off?

A: Read Nolan. Thanks!

NANCY HOLDER

Nancy Holder is a multiple award-winning, *New York Times* bestselling author (the *Wicked* series). Her two new dark young adult dark fantasy series are *Crusade* and *Wolf Springs Chronicles*. She has won five Bram Stoker Awards from the Horror Writers Association, as well as a Scribe Award for Best Novel (*Saving Grace: Tough Love*.) Nancy has sold over eighty novels and one hundred short stories, many of them based on such shows as *Highlander, Buffy the Vampire Slayer, Angel*, and others. She lives in San Diego with her daughter, Belle, two corgis, and three cats.

You can visit Nancy online at: nancyholder.com

Q: With your experience with YA literature, how do you know where to draw the line; where there may be too much grit or too much of an edge to a story?

A: This is a tough decision, and I find that the older my daughter gets, the more circumspect I become. She's fifteen now. The *Wicked* series is very dark; *Crusade* has dealt a lot with matters of faith and is far less brutal. *Unleashed* is the least dark of the three, and the most recent. Sometimes adult readers object to underage drinking, language, or sex. I don't believe that you have to do certain things you feel are inappropriate because "the story demanded it." But this is a tough question for me to answer right now. My daughter is sitting across from me chuckling because I was taken aback that someone wrote "fucking awesome" in a book review for *Damned*, the second book in the *Crusade* series. I swear all the time, but I have these little pockets of anxiety when I'm around her.

Q: Do you think parents are as concerned about what their kids are reading as much as what they are watching?

A: The parents I know, yes. Most of the moms read *Twilight* first. And a lot of my daughter's friends don't even watch TV.

Q: DreamWorks has picked up *Wicked*, which you co-wrote with Debbie Vigue. How is that going?

A: We've gone into turn around. But our agency is still very excited about it and we've learned that *Wicked* never dies.

Q: Do you feel that your early *Buffy* novels had an effect on YA genre fiction?

A: I think Joss Whedon had an effect on YA genre fiction. I think he made it hip to be honest and smart. I think he showed that heroes can fail badly, and still be heroes. I was lucky enough and honored enough to work with his characters, but he deserves the credit.

Q: What do you think of the current state of genre TV? *The Walking Dead*, for example. (Although it's adapted from a graphic novel)?

A: I'm so happy that there's lots of genre on right now. It's a feast of fantasy and dark fantasy. Long may it wave.

Q: Every time someone says the vampire is a dead character, somebody comes along and rejuvenates it. Zombies are the hips thing now, have been for a while…Do you think they'll fade?

A: I don't know. I've been surprised by their longevity, but why should I be? They're zombies. I wrote my first zombie short story in 1992 ("Passion Play") and I just did a piece of Stephen Jones' zombie trilogy. So the bubble hasn't burst yet.

Q: There are plenty of places for strong female characters in the genre, we had Buffy, Sonja Blue, and characters like Domino Lady. What does it take to create a successful character that resonates with fans as much as those have?

A: One thing that I've noticed is that because there's not as much history and context about strong women characters, they're taken to task for things we let slide with our comic book superheroes.. Domino Lady fights crime in stilettos and she carries sleeping powder, knockout drops, a hypodermic needle, a Saturday Night Special, and calling cards. Artists are always asking me where she keeps all this stuff even after I mention that there's a pouch in her cape. Why she's wearing heels. Because she's a crime-fighting adventuress, that's why!

Q: Where did the concept for the Domino Lady come from? She's rather esoteric in a fan way.

A: The Domino Lady is a pulp character from the 1930s. She only appeared in six stories but she's such a vixen that her story has continued. She was only one of a handful of sassy dames who did the things bazillions of male pulp characters did.

Q: When you wrote *The Screaming Season*, you watched a horror movie every morning during the writing of it. Could you name a few?
A: *A Tale of Two Sisters; El Orfanato*; all the *Ring* versions, Japanese and American; same with *Grudge: The Others; The Innocents; The Haunting; The Shining; Memento Mori*; lots and lots of J-horror. *Kwaidan*.

Q: Did watching them in the morning affect the tone of the storytelling?

A: I watched movies and listened to horror movie soundtracks until I felt scared. Then I tried to stay scared all day. If it started to wear off, I watched a couple of key scenes from *A Tale of Two Sisters*, which is on my computer. I couldn't watch any of these movies after dark because I couldn't sleep if I did!

Q: Do you have any other writing habits like the horror movies?

A: I write to music whenever I can. I have tons and tons of horror soundtracks and I listen to them constantly while I'm working. I just finished a *Teen Wolf* novel. The new TV show is fabulous and I can't wait for the next season. It's sexy and scary, funny, and involving. They tell you all the music that's used in very accessibly playlists—*Teen Wolf* is on MTV, so duh! I'm so glad I got approached about writing the book because I probably wouldn't have watched it. I'm getting ready to write a dark nursery rime for *Two And Twenty*, edited by Georgia McBride and company. My nurse rhyme is "The Lion and the Unicorn," about the accession of James VI of Scotland to the English throne. And I'm super excited to announce that I've been working on a Buffy coffee table book. It's going to be gorgeous.

Q: A lot of the horror genre has relied on stoking the fires of simple fears, sometimes ones from childhood. They continue to resonate with readers and watchers over and over again. Why do you suppose we have still have yet to outgrow the Thing From Under the Bed?

A: I think those kinds of fears are so primal that they live in the reptilian brain, and we can't get rid of them ever. They're as much a part of us as our DNA. Lucky for us horror writers.

Q: How do you choose an author to collaborate with? (And yes, you can take that as a completely unveiled attempt to get your attention)

A: Again, may I saw how gallant you are. I'm friends with a lot of writers and if I think we might be compatible to work on something, I suggest it. With Debbie Viguié, she was a student of mine at the Maui Writers Conference. Her talent was blazing. I needed someone to help me write *Wicked* and Debbie was the one. We've just celebrated our tenth year writing together, and we've sold eleven novels and one short story. Debbie also has her own career, as I do mine. As I'm writing this to you, I'll be seeing her in about 7 hours for breakfast at Gallifrey One, a Dr. Who convention, here in L.A. She flew out from Orlando to be here and I can't wait to see her.

Q: Last question; how would you like your tombstone to read?

A: SHE WAS A GOOD WRITER AND A GREAT MOM.

TAD WILLIAMS

Tad Williams has held more jobs than any sane person should admit to—singing in a band, selling shoes, managing a financial institution, throwing newspapers, and designing military manuals, to name just a few. He also hosted a syndicated radio show for ten years, worked in theater and television production, taught both grade-school and college classes, and worked in multimedia for a major computer firm. He is co-founder of an interactive television company, and is currently writing comic books and film and television scripts as well as novels.

Tad and his wife, Deborah Beale, live in the San Francisco Bay Area with their children and far more cats, dogs, turtles, pet ants and banana slugs than they can count.

Q: *The Dragons of Ordinary Farm* was co-written with your wife. How was the experience of not only collaborating with your wife, but writing a story for younger readers?

A: Collaborating with anyone is interesting, but collaborating with a spouse is even more so. Deb and I are very different in our habits and approach so it's been a challenge, but I've loved having the chance to work on something with her.

Q: What can you tell us about the sequel, *The Secrets of Ordinary Farm?*

A: It elaborates on the events in the first book, answering some questions and raising some new ones, but there's also a whole adventure that begins and ends in this volume, so even if you haven't read the first you can enjoy this one.

Q: What was it like penning comics for D.C. Comics?

A: I've always loved comics, so getting to write some was fun. I would have liked to have taken a longer shot at *Aquaman*, but that wasn't the way it worked out. That was my only real frustration. But just being able to set some things up that I hope future *Aquaman* writers will use—way cool.

Q: Will you take readers back to Osten Ard?

A: I plan to, if not in the exact ways they expect. I'd like to do a collection of short stories, tied together by a central framing story. I've been waiting to get to that for years, so we'll see...

Q: For many of us, *Tailchaser's Song* holds a special place for us, given that it was published some time ago (1985), do you have the same feelings for it now as you did then?

A: It's so far back I can barely remember the me who wrote it, but of course it's my first book and will always be a sentimental favorite. It's being made into an animated film by a company called Animetropolis, which is very exciting.

Q: Given the current state of printed books, chains like Borders closing, and the rise of e-readers, what do you think the fate of the bookstore or the printed page will be in say, ten or twenty years?

A: I suspect regular paper books will become more and more of a prestige item—something for collectors and lovers of fine work. More and more people will be reading electronically. That said, I don't think old-fashioned books will disappear, anymore than acoustic instruments did after synthesizers came along.

Q: What went in to the decision to publish *Shadowmarch* exclusively online?

A: I just wanted to do something different and I was interested in both the internet and the concept of serialization. I'm still interested in both. Maybe I'll do another online novel one of these days.

Q: *Shadowmarch* is clearly a universe that can expand to no real set end. Can you tell us about what's next?

A: I've just finished my next book, *The Dirty Streets of Heaven*, the first of three (but not a trilogy, because they're also meant to stand on their own) about Bobby Dollar, an earthbound angel caught up in the cold war between Heaven and Hell. I'm really enjoying them. They're a bit more adult than my other books—more sex and swearing—but they're also funny (I think) and will be fun to read. Lots of monsters, demons, and weird ideas.

Q: Do the villains in your books, say Johnny Dread, think of themselves as villains? Do you approach the creation of antagonist differently than protagonist?

A: Everybody is the hero of his or her own story. That includes villains. Hitler didn't think, "How can I screw up the world?," he thought, "How can I make the world perfect for people like me?" Same result, but that illustrates the difference in approach. Sadly, most villains either think they're heroes—which would be Ineluki in my *MS&T* books—or are sociopaths who don't care about anyone else, which would be Dread. Either way, they don't spend a lot of time wondering how their opponents see them.

Q: What made you write the Christmas story, "The Sugarplum Favor?"

A: Had an idea and it was a few days before Christmas so I thought it would be fun. I like writing short, and if I've got a chance I'll knock one out. I'd like to do more.

Q: How much of you is in your characters?
A little of me is in all of them, and there's a lot of me in some—Renie Sulaweyo, Prince Josua. I try to use what I know, so almost every character is going to be tested against my own personal truth—"if this was me, would I act this way?" It means putting oneself in some strange shoes occasionally.

Q: Has there been any interest to have your books adapted to film?

A: Besides the aforementioned *Tailchaser* animated film, the *Otherland* books have been optioned for a film. I don't have much information about it yet, except that the producer has done good work and seems to get things done. Fingers crossed.

Q: You've mentioned you'd like to work with George R. R. Martin. Has that come any closer to being a reality?

A: George and I are both pretty busy. Maybe when he finishes his current story (hah!) we'll find a chance to do something.

Q: How does the creative process start for you?

A: There's no set rule. Ideas bounce around in the back of my mind. Those with staying power usually begin to create or draw other ideas, combining and growing until I can't avoid them any longer. Then I begin to think about whether I want to do something more concrete with them. If they last through that process, they join the line of things I mean to turn into books or stories.

KATHE KOJA

While she is a prolific author of short stories, most of her short fiction remains uncollected. Koja's novels and short stories frequently concern characters who have been in some way marginalized by society, often focusing on the transcendence and/or disintegration which proceeds from this social isolation (as in *The Cipher*, *Bad Brains*, "Teratisms," *The Blue Mirror*, etc.). Koja won the Bram Stoker Award and the Locus Award for her first novel *The Cipher*, and a Deathrealm Award for *Strange Angels*.

Kathe can be found online at: kathekoja.com

Q: You've swung between YA and Horror. Have there been any troubles in your publishing one or the other because of your previous work?

A: I started out writing SF, then moved into horror, contemporary fiction, YA, and now with *Under The Poppy* and its sequel, *The Mercury Waltz*, historical fiction. To me the concept of genre is like attending a party of gorgeous strangers—who will you meet there, what fun will you have? So far, no one has given me the bum's rush from any of the parties based on my attendance at any of the others.

Q: Would it be fair to call your Horror work as 'Splatterpunk?'

A: Some people have (and do), but I don't.

Q: What's the last book you read?

A: *Puppet: An Essay On Uncanny Life* by Kenneth Gross. Mysterious, emotional, and involving; I highly recommend it. I've just started reading David McCullough's *The Greater Journey: Americans In Paris*—really good stuff.

For fiction, I'm a judge for this year's Ferro-Grumley awards, so I'm reading the list there. No comments, of course, till the judging is done, but I've definitely found a couple of bylines to cherish.

Q: Your YA Fiction seems to attract the 'Emo' kind of crowd rather than the somewhat geeky crowd that 'Harry Potter' captured. Do you think that's accurate?

A: I'm not sure—a book finds its reader, and vice versa, in ways that stay at times inside the bounds of previous taste, and sometimes not at all. That's why I'm always flummoxed when a parent asks me at an event, "Which of your books will my daughter/son/nephew/godchild like?" How in the world could I know that?

Q: Does your inspiration for writing come from one constant source, or does it differ from work to work?

A: Everything I do starts with an image—for *Under The Poppy*, it was a man, a performer, on the road with his troupe of *outre* puppets; for *Buddha Boy* it was a boy in a wild t-shirt, looking down a stairwell at another boy below.

The image intrigues me, I start to learn more about it, other images accrete around it—and sometimes, a book results. Not always, but sometimes.

And writing itself is pretty much the way I live in the world: I have to write, I love to write.

Q: What kind of feedback have you received from your younger fans?

A: Honest, heartfelt, perspicacious, and humbling.

Q: You adapted *Under the Poppy* to a stage show. What went into the adaptation of it?

A: An enormous amount of work! So far, we've done three Poppy events—the first at Motor City Pride, the second called "The Company We Keep" during the People's Art Festival, and "Love is a Puppet" as part of "Victorian Opulence" at District VII Detroit.

The first was an introduction to the concept of the Poppy, the next two were the story of Istvan on the road, and this performance takes us into the world of the Poppy itself, with floozies, love, and darkness—and multimedia accoutrements. And yes, there will definitely be puppets ...

Each is part of the whole narrative of the Poppy story, and each builds on the last, onward to the full event, which will be immersive and all-encompassing. It's an amazing and exciting way to retell the story, and so much more fun than plunking an audience into seats and saying "Just sit there and watch."

Q: You worked with Joe Stacey on the music of the stage show. What made you choose him and what went into the collaboration?

A: Joe Stacey and I met through a mutual friend (hi, Aaron!), when the book trailer for *Under The Poppy* was being created. I gave Joe the lyrics and a few vague ideas, and he knocked it out of the park.

http://www.underthepoppy.com/under-the-poppy-the-trailer

We began talking about the larger show, I gave Joe a working version of the script, and again, he created amazing work: "All the World Loves a Lover," "Is It Real"—and scored what will be the projections/visuals for the show, too. Joe is a fantastic performer as well as a composer, and he plans to play live in that show.

Most recently, we worked together on the book trailer for the ebook release of my first novel, *The Cipher*, coming this spring. Joe had read the book, saw the first edit of the film (yes, we shot on real film), and yet again, came up with something memorable, fierce and otherworldly. It's a privilege to work with someone so talented.

Q: One of the most compelling story devices in *Under The Poppy* is the use of rather unique puppets. What inspired you to use them?

A: They are rather unique, indeed, and some of them even anatomically correct ... Again, I saw Istvan on the road, this performer with his troupe of four actors, *les mecs*; then I saw another man, Rupert, and knew that they loved one another; and I followed them both from there.

The puppet as character/actor in a novel is a wonderful construct, because there's nothing a puppet can't do, become, or represent. The more I read and learn about puppets, the more I respect them.

Q: Is there a type of genre you'd like to write that you haven't yet?

A: I would love to do a picture book with very few words. A very difficult and demanding process, like haiku. Maybe someday.

Q: I've had two cats, both rescues, and so a work like *Straydog* has a particular resonance for me. Was there a particular reason you wrote it?

A: I'm so pleased to hear about your rescues, and to know that *Straydog* spoke to you—all of our cats are rescues, too. I do volunteer work for some animal rescue agencies, and that experience certainly went into the story, but I didn't consciously say "I'm going to write about the plight of feral animals." There was an image: a girl with a notebook, who turned out to be Rachel, and Grrl, the dog she loves and tries to rehab.

And *Straydog* was a short story at first, called "straydog," that I wrote for *Cicada* magazine, and that my agent, Christopher Schelling, suggested I might want to expand into a novel: "There's a lot more there," he said, and he was right.

Q: Do young women approach you for advice on anything because of your YA work?

A: You mean writing, or life? The first I'm qualified to expound on, at least from one particular perspective, and I enjoy talking to younger writers more than any other group in the world. The second is a different matter and one I would be very careful about.

Q: Was it difficult to switch from an 'adult' genre to YA?

A: Nope.

Q: Is there a particular novel in the Horror genre that to you, defines the word Horror?

A: There are horror novels I love to go back to—*Dracula*, Shirley Jackson's *Hill House*, *The Shining*—and some of M.R. James' short fiction that, no matter how many times I read it, continue to frighten and disturb me: not with what might be happening in the darkness, but what is.

Q: What is currently happening with the film version of *The Cipher*?

A: The film version of *Cipher* is in the develo ment phase—the production team is nailing down the script, working on financing, attaching talent, and so on. Hollywood is its own terrain, but I have great confidence in the team's vision and passion for the project—and its smarts. I'll share more news on my blog as it happens.

Q: I enjoyed Kink for its approach of a normal person in a decidedly unreal situation and the subtext of the human condition or am I reading too much into that?

A: I hope everything I write has that subtext—it's our terrain, as readers and writers. Though *Kink's* always been called "contemporary fiction," to me it's a horror novel, as is *Going Under*, one of my YAs, and for the same reason: the depiction of human need and greed as a black hole of selfishness that recognizes no boundaries, and counts no one as its equal.

The landscape of hell.

Q: *Skin*, to me, was an unflinching look at what I suppose could be called an alternative lifestyle, but very dark and humorless. Was it planned that way or did the spine of the story dictate it could be no other way?

A: When *Skin* was published, in 1993, some people on reading it were amazed that anyone could want to actually piece himself/herself at all, and why in the world would anyone write, or read, about such a weird and fringey culture? Recently someone showed me a reader's comment on *Skin* that said "Oh, piercing is so dull and *passé*, everyone's been there done that!" To me, that's pretty humorous.

Q: You¹ve that in Headlong, you were most like the character of Hazel. Who are you like in say, *Skin* or *Under the Poppy?*

A: It's definitely hard for me to think in those terms—I believe an interviewer posed me a strict either-or on Hazel and Lily. :) The characters in the novels are who they are, not modeled after anyone, including me. If I'm anyone in *Under the Poppy*, it would probably be Pan Loudermilk.

Q: Was YA a genre that was as clearly defined when you were a teen as it isnow? Would you say the genre is clearly defined?
A: In a marketing sense it means one thing, to an individual reader it means another; there are some adult readers who won't pick up anything labeled YA, sadly.

But back in the day there was no shelf for books specifically meant to explore the years of adolescence—there were children's books, and then there were adult books. S.E. Hinton is a golden exception, and there were a few voices out there, but nothing like the deluge now. A golden age for YA readers, whatever their own chronology.

Q: What can we look forward to in the future from you?

A: I hope pleasure and surprise . . . *Under the Poppy* will be out in paperback this fall, *The Mercury Waltz* early in 2013. I'm working on another book but it's too early to talk about. The *Under the Poppy* show is projected for fall 2012, in Detroit; come and see! And I'm planning a work on the poet and playwright Christopher Marlowe, but what form that will eventually take is still a mystery. I love mysteries.

TOM PICCIRILLI

Tom Piccirilli is the author of more than twenty novels including: *The Last Kind Words, Shadow Season, The Cold Spot, The Coldest Mile,* and *A Choir of Ill Children*. He's won two International Thriller Awards and four Bram Stoker Awards, as well as having been nominated for the Edgar, the World Fantasy Award, the Macavity, and Le Grand Prix de l'Imaginaire.

Tom's website is: www.thecoldspot.blogspot.com

Q: With *Every Shallow Cut,* your narrative is sometimes stream-of consciousness, and other times erratic. Did you have any particular problems in writing it because of this style?

A: I think that's how most of us live our lives, so it was a more natural mirror for an authentic personality of someone on the edge. His mind wanders, he drifts through life, he thinks about the past, fears and anger and frustrations constantly tug at his attention. So it was easier to write if anything because a writer is always trying to give the impression of a character's natural mental state. Writing the story and backstory at the same time just allowed me to create a more fully sympathetic and understandable protagonist.

Q: I've noticed that a lot of Horror-based authors such as yourself tend to go into writing Crime or Noir novels. What's the attraction?

A: Horror seems like a young man's game to me. It's full of fantasy and uproots the reader from full realism. But the older a writer gets I think the more authentic and realistic topics he finds to write about. The topics are still dark, and the basic conflict remains good versus evil, but crime/noir seems to focus our perception inward and backward, rather than outward and forward. They are stories of personal character, personal fears, disappointments, regrets, needs, and the grays of life, rather than the more obvious black versus white, good and bad, details of circumstance rather than of enduring life.

Q: I enjoyed the novella *You'd Better Watch Out*. What made you choose the first-person narrative in a book about a young man from a tragically broken home to become a hitman with some serious demons to deal with?

A: Because first person was the more immediate way to tell the story. I wanted readers to understand t his guy who was a very complex protagonist. He was evil, in his way, but I wanted readers to sympathize with him, and so I had to show his background, the terrible events of his childhood, and show how he was, in effect, created from these circumstances and incidents, how he lived with them, how he released them.

Q: What are your feelings about the Horror genre as it stands today?

A: I hardly read any nowadays. Most of it doesn't feel very real to me. It deals with subject matter that doesn't interest me much. Like I said, I prefer realistic fiction to the more fantastical sort. Maybe the wheel will turn again and I'll start reading more horror, fantasy, and science fiction again, which are the genres that made me first fall in love with reading when I was a kid. But as it stands, I read primarily crime fiction and non-fiction at the moment.

Q: I have to admit, I loved the title of your work, *Fuckin' Lie Down Already*. Jack Ketchum was quoted as saying, "This is a small masterpiece. It's said that the devil's in the details and Tom got all the details exactly right. I always said Pic was one to watch. Fuck watching. He's utterly there. A voice to listen to and learn from." Does that kind of praise change your mindset while writing?

A: It was very generous of him to provide that blurb, but positive reviews/praise/criticism, none of it tends to change my mind set at this point of the game. I have my voice, I have my material, I have the themes and wells of creativity from which I draw. The writing is its own creature. It feeds itself, it goes places that I might not necessarily want to go or even understand. The act is a kind of fusion of conscious will and desire and unconscious need and driving force.

Q: *The Last Kind Words* follows the dynamics of someone being raised in less than ideal circumstances. Why is that such a powerful element for you to use?

A: Backstory is story. History is what brings us to the present, it makes us who we are. Drama and conflict are what make darker characters darker in the first place. It's more interesting for a protagonist to have to go through some kind of traumatic event or events as a kid. We've all had them, we've all suffered through them, and they leave their scars and their marks. We live with those scars and those demons. They follow us, they are us. Drama is the pearl built from the grain of sand of pain.

Q: Which of your books would you recommend new readers to start with?

A: *LKW* is my most recent novel and seems to reflect who I am as a writer at the moment. We're all always changing and all always learning, but everything I've learned as a writer has gone into that novel. It's very representational of me as a person. My sense of humor, my regrets, my disappointments, the great motifs of myself.

Q: As a fan of Asian cinema, what drew you to that particular style?

A: Asian cinema seems to embrace all manners of kinks and oddity and uniqueness. They understand the greater circumference of life. Their movies are totally insane, way over the top, but honest, at a primal and basic level. There's less need to project perfection or heroism the way American cinema seems to do. Here, we're so terrified of always providing good examples. In Asian cinema, it's enough just to try to tell an honest story about flawed people, sad people, driven people.

Q: You have over twenty books to your credit, and have won the Stoker and the International Thriller Writer's Award. Looking back, did those achievements happen as fast as they seem to have?

A: They don't seem very fast to me. In a 100 word bio they might add up quickly, but we all know that is distilled from the grinding of life. You work. You keep working. You put out product. You tell one story after the next. Sometimes people like what you do and there's some validation along the way, awards, praise, or other kindnesses. But just like every Joe doing his job every day, you do it because you have to do it, because it's the job to do, and the accolades are few and far between.

Q: I once heard Harlan Ellison say that it's more important to be a plumber than a writer. Do you agree?

A: In a manner of speaking, sure. When the house is flooding, you don't need some creative outlet. You don't need to read a book or watch a movie. You need to get somebody over to your house to fix a busted septic pipe right now. Art is a necessity but it's also recreational, it's food for the soul. It's not an immediate necessity like some other things might be. And so a writer isn't as important as some other jobs might be in certain circumstances.

Q: To me, your writing is reliably dark without always having to resort to blow-by-blow dismemberment. How do you establish this as an author? Does the voice of the Horror or Crime fan speak up and guide you so to speak?

A: It's all about emotional context, not the hacking off of limbs. We all have to face our dark nights of the soul. Tragedies, social terrors, personal upsets. You show the darkness by understanding the darkness, our shared darkness. Writing is all about finding common ground between the writer and the reader. The insider and the outsider. A writer gambles that he knows his audience, that the audience is, in fact, very much like himself. I'm guessing that I can tell stories full of enough elements that hit you in the same way they hit me. Whether that's drama or humor or horror or whatever, that's the whole objective. A stand-up comic tells his jokes because he figures you'll understand his observations. You'll have seen similar things, you'll look at the world the same way he does. We have the same basic understanding of the world at large.

Q: *The Last Kind Words* resonated with me not only because of the dynamic storytelling, but because of its portrayal of the human condition. Was that something you intentionally used as a thread, or was it just in the subtext of the story and the characters in it?

A: Well, I don't know how you write without somehow dealing with the human condition. What else is writing? So, sure, it was intentional, I don't know how you talk about humanity as subtext, by accident in fiction, without intending to do so. In any case, as mentioned earlier, I'm always trying to find common ground, to draw the reader in because these are subjects and themes and context that we all share. If something disappoints or frustrates me, then chances are it'll do the same to you. The "story" as such is just to propel the commentary about all the other stuff that goes along with it. The story is the smallest part of the tale, if that makes any sense. It's the discussion on life and love and poetry and pain that's the real steam that drives the engine.

Q: What are you working on now?

A: A sequel to *LKW* and a number of other projects. Novellas of one sort or another, new short stories, and a couple of standalone novels in various states of completion.

KEVIN J. ANDERSON

Kevin's got the envious status of having forty bestsellers. He has written spin-off novels for *Star Wars*, *StarCraft*, *Titan A.E.*, and *The X-Files*, and with Brian Herbert is the co-author of the *Dune* prequels. His original works include the *Saga of Seven Suns* series and the Nebula Award-nominated Assemblers of Infinity. Some of Anderson's superhero novels include *Enemies & Allies*, about the first meeting of Batman and Superman and *The Last Days of Krypton*, telling the story of how Krypton came to be destroyed and the choice two parents had to make for their son.

Q: You stepped into a pair of large shoes when you took up the *Dune* series with Brian Herbert. What was involved in becoming part of that legacy?

A: We told the story in detail in an Author's Note in *House Atreides*. It's been close to 15 years ago now, when Brian and I first made contact. I had always been a huge *Dune* fan, and Frank Herbert had left his great chronicles unfinished. Brian was a successful writer in his own right, and I had plenty of credentials. Together, we used our love for *Dune*, studying the original novels, and a lot of Frank Herbert's notes to carry on the story. The recently released *Sisterhood of Dune* is our twelfth novel together in the series.

Q: I enjoyed the novel *Enemies and Allies*, which featured Batman and Superman. How did you approach creating the story for these iconic characters?

A: I had already done my first DC Universe novel *The Last Days of Krypton*, which got me fully immersed in the Superman saga, but when I delved into *Enemies & Allies* I tried to get into who the characters were as *people* in the real world, Clark Kent trying to be a normal guy knowing he's a great superhero......but Bruce Wayne, I think, really considers himself as a dark vigilante and only pretends to be a rich socialite.

Q: What comic book character would you like to write about?

A: Already done! Batman and Superman would have been my first picks.

Q: *Terra Incognita* shows a world that features very few of the expected tropes one may expect from Fantasy; very little magic or Conan-like characters on epic quests for the Chalice of the Great Something. It's all very organic; Was there a conscious effort on your part to sort of step away from the accepted norm of the genre?

A: I was inspired by the legend of Prester John and his great land across the sea. I didn't want to write a fantasy with bearded wizards waving magic wands; in *Terra Incognita* there are sea serpents, but they're just scary animals. However, there is some magic, and unexplored landscapes, and great quests, which gave me the ability to explore real gritty religious conflicts and intolerance--in a way that would be more demonstrative than if I used real countries and real conflicts. It's more of a historical epic, but set in an imaginary land.

Q: What motivated you to have a soundtrack composed for *Terra Incognita*?

A: The two rock CDs are actually more like crossover albums, telling part of the story in a rock-opera fashion. Much of my writing had been influenced by music--Kansas, Rush, etc.--and because the record producer and label owner of ProgRock Records was a fan of mine, we had the opportunity to do something innovative, with a rock CD and a novel written by the same author. And I think both turned out very well, it was a great experience to work on.

Q: You've written over one hundred novels at this point, having seen your first novel *Resurrection, Inc.* at the age of twenty-five. That's quite a feat. To what do you attribute not only the sheer number, but your continued success?

A: I love to write. I love to tell stories, and I keep thinking of stories—I never get tired of it. All I've ever wanted to be was a writer, and I work hard so I don't have to find a different career!

Q: You've played in the universes of the likes of Chris Carter, George Lucas, and Frank Herbert. Are there any other 'prefab' universes you'd like to participate in?

A: I am a writer, but I'm also a fanboy at heart, so I loved the movies, TV shows, and classics of the genre. Right now my plate is so full of projects that I really love, I can't think of anything I'd rather be doing. If only there were more hours in the day, and at the keyboard.

Q: Your short story, "Prisoner of War" is a sequel to Harlan Ellison's "Soldier" from *The Outer Limits*. How did you come to write that, and was Harlan involved at all?

A: When I approached Harlan with the idea, he was initially skeptical, said he never had any interest in doing sequels to something he had already written, in fact saw no point in them. Then I pointed out to him that he had created a fascinating and complex universe for "Soldier"—So, Harlan, are you saying that there's only *one* possible story to tell in that whole universe? So he decided to let me take a crack at it. He provided the introduction and his original script to "Soldier" and I wrote the sequel story "Prisoner of War." [The original book publication with Harlan's part, *Outer Limits: Armageddon Dreams*, is very rare and hard to find!]

Q: What went into the process of the current *Dune* novel, *Sisterhood of Dune*?

A: This one is the origin of the Bene Gesserit Sisterhood a few decades after the Battle of Corrin. Since this is the 12th one, Brian and I have our process down and we know what each person is supposed to do. It was very smooth.

Q: How many more *Dune* novels can we expect from you and Brian?
A: *Sisterhood* is the first of a trilogy, so we have two more of those, and we've got our own original *Hellhole* trilogy to wrap up—that maps out the next five years or so.

Q: I've always enjoyed the stories of Jules Verne, so naturally I was drawn to your *Captain Nemo*, which covers a considerable amount of backstory for a classic literary character. What went into the writing of it?

A: I loved that book! It's one of my favorites of all my novels. I grew up reading Jules Verne, and *Captain Nemo* allowed me to reread all those classic novels, tie together all the Verneian story threads, and create my own homage. *Captain Nemo* took me more than three years to research and write, and I am very pleased with how it turned out.

Q: What are your five 'desert island' books?

A: *Lonesome Dove* by Larry McMurtry, *Dune* by Frank Herbert, *Lord of the Rings* by Tolkien, and then I'll probably toss in two books from my "To Read" stack, so I have something new and fresh to read.

Q: Are there any of your fellow *Star Wars* author whom you especially admire?

A: I worked closely with a great many of the *SW* writers and comic writers when I was working on my novels. Dave Wolverton, Mike Stackpole, Timothy Zahn, Tom Veitch, and the artists Dave Dorman and Christian Gossett. We were all part of a very fun team at Lucasfilm—some of the most fun I've ever had.

Q: Which one of your characters would you like to have a long dinner conversation with and what would be served?

A: I think that would have to be Captain Nemo...and we'd probably have steak, because he's probably tired of seafood!

Q: *Hellhole* is a novel you wrote with Brian Herbert that was your own collaborative creation. What was the collaborative process like to build that particular world?

A: We had worked so well together on 11 *Dune* novels, so it was time to try our hand at a universe of our own creation. We had created many different planets, histories, and characters in *Dune*, so we were well prepped to create *Hellhole*. It took a lot of brainstorming, character building, and plotting. We're just finishing the second novel in the trilogy now, and are still building the universe.

Q: Anything you'd like to end with?

A: Just to point out that we're releasing many of our out-of-print and hard-to-find titles as eBooks—including many Frank Herbert titles—at wordfirepress.com. It's a new opportunity to put classic works back into print.

STORM CONSTANTINE

Storm Constantine is an internationally-published author of over thirty books, both fiction and non-fiction. She is the founder of Immanion Press, originally created to keep her back catalogue of novels in print, but which now publishes many other authors. Best known for her Wraeththu novels, involving an androgynous and powerful race of beings that arise from humanity, Storm has also written non-fiction titles, some of which are available from Immanion Press. Storm is also a teacher of creative writing, an editor and a Reiki Teacher, among many other interests.

Q: You were brought up reading mythology rather than genre Fantasy. What sort of effect do you think that has had on your work?

A: There wasn't an awful lot of genre fantasy available when I was very young, certainly not for children, so mythology was the most fantastical literature I had available to me. The stories inspired me and I loved to create 'sequels' to the old legends. In a way it was a kind of mythology fan fiction!

Q: What can you tell us about the magical work that you've done?

A: I could write a book on that, so it's difficult to paraphrase. I've delved into many aspects of magic over the years, and I suppose the culmination of all this exploration and learning was creating my own magical systems, such as Deharan Magic and the healing system Sekhem Heka. I love pop culture magic and creating new systems. I suppose it goes with my whole bundle of creative urges generally.

Q: What was the road that led you to using hermaphroditic and androgynous figures in your work?

A: It goes back a long way, but I can't say when the exact moment was that I became interested in the androgyne as a magical creature. I wrote stories and poems about proto-Wraeththu way back in my teens.

Q: There have been Tantric touches in your work and explorations of the energy it creates. What caused you to explore the element of sex magic? Is it more symbolic than literal?

A: Everything I write just emerges from me without any conscious decisions being made over content. Quite often people read meaning into my work that wasn't put there deliberately, but patterns emerge in a novel that seemingly have a life of their own. I've always regarded sex as sacred, so it disappoints me that for many it is meaningless beyond basic gratification. With the Wraeththu books, I explored sexuality as a magical force.

Q: You've said that vampirism is a metaphor for oral sex and a kind of Russian roulette when it comes to dealing with the fangy types. What would you say creatures like say, the werewolf, are symbolic of?
A: To me it is simply the beast within. We are all werewolves at heart. It's just that some choose not to show it!

Q: I may be getting off track here, but as you've referred to things such as the Dead Sea Scrolls being an inspiration, have you read such things as *The Gospel of Judas*?

A: No, I haven't read that particular text.

Q: What is your muse?

A: She's a capricious beast who sometimes takes protracted holidays for no good reason!

Q: What have been some of your most memorable paranormal experiences?

A: These stories are all too long to relate here, because they'd need to be told in context. Let's just say I've experienced some inexplicable stuff over the years. Whenever I meet someone new, one of the first things I like to ask them when there's chance for a good long chat is 'what's the weirdest thing that ever happened to you?' It's amazing how many bizarre stories come out, from the most unlikely people.

Q: Where does your passion for Egypt come from?

A: It's been with me since before I went to school. My first ever story concerned a fox who went back to ancient Egypt. I think I was affected deeply by the Bast scene in *The Three Lives of Thomasina*, which in all other respects is a rather cheesy old Disney (I think) film. But there is this one scene where the cat 'dies' and goes to the goddess, only to be reborn. That was it for me I think. I was obsessed by cat-headed women as a child and made up lots of stories about them. I imagined being one: her name was Rhodora and she had a blue mane.

Q: What made you create your own publishing company, Immanion Press?

At first it was simply to bring my Wraeththu books back into print—the original trilogy—and to provide a UK publication for the second trilogy. It just grew from there.

Q: One of the classes you've taught was called 'Tarot Without Tears.' Could you explain the meaning of the title?

A: There's no great meaning to it really. It just refers to the fact that there is a lot of memorizing to do with learning to read Tarot, so it can be rather a chore. The system I use to teach it involves mnemonics to help people learn quickly.

Q: Are there any plans to publish your artwork in a collection?

A: Not at the moment, because I have so many other projects on the go. I might consider it in future.

Q: What went into the world-building of *The Wraeththu Histories*?

A: Not a great deal to begin with! I was more obsessed with the characters than their environment, but over time, I fleshed out the world and gave it a firmer foundation. When I released the 'author's cut' versions of the original trilogy I put some of this material into the books to make them stronger.

Q: One of the most striking books of yours to me is Mythangelus. What inspired you to pursue angelic themes such as those?

A: I have always been intrigued by angels, but distinctly not the fluffy kind. Over the years various story ideas have come to me, and I collected them together in that particular anthology. When I brought out the four story collections I attempted to put those with a similar theme together as much as possible, although there was inevitably some overlap. One story, "The Oracle Lips," actually found its way into two of the collections, completely by accident. I didn't realize this until a reviewer pointed it out!

Q: Did you layer in Pagan-based worship in *Sea Dragon Air*, or was it you built for the people to believe in?

A: The religious systems in the *Magravandias* trilogy were created for the story. I didn't regard any of them as being "Pagan" (in a modern sense) as such. It was a fantasy world, and those were simply the beliefs held by its inhabitants.

Q: Do you feel the success of books like *Sign of the Sacred*, and *Hermetech*, overwhelm works like *Magranadias* series?

A: Yes, to a degree. It's particularly noticeable in the ebooks I've brought out. The *Wraeththu* books are the most popular, followed by the *Grigori* trilogy, then *The Thorn Boy*, the Magravandias story collection. *Burying the Shadow*, *Hermetech* and *Thin Air* are also available as ebooks but they don't perform as well as the others. There are still a number of books I've yet to republish through Immanion, and these will also become ebooks eventually. I only got the rights back for the *Magravandias* books last year.

Q: How did you come to work with Michael Moorcock on *Silverheart?*

A: He had a first draft for the book and didn't have the time to complete it, so asked me to do so.

Q: What do you do to relax?

A: Listen to music, watch movies, play World of Warcraft, spend time with friends.

Q: Your last non-fiction book was 2008's *Sekhem Heka: A Natural Healing and Self Development System*. Will we be seeing any more NF from you?

A: I'm currently working on the second book of the Deharan Magic system, *Grimore Dehara: Ulani*. This is co-authored with Daniel Marcheschi, with input from his Nayati forum members and also the Wraeththu magical group in Second Life. There's a lot of fascinating material out there now, from people who began working with the system when the first book came out. The second book will include some of this material.

Q: What are you working on now? Anything to promote, rant, or talk about?

A: Apart from the *Grimoire Dehara* I just mentioned, I'm also in the process of compiling two more anthologies. The first is the second Wraeththu Mythos short story collection, called *Para Imminence*. This will include at least one new story from me, and hopefully two—if I get the time.

The second is a sequel to *What a Long Strange, Trip It's Been*, which was an anthology of articles and stories about *World of Warcraft*. I'm currently taking submissions for both of these books if anyone is interested in contributing. There are guidelines available. People can mail info@immanion-press.com to ask for them.

I have a short story to write for an anthology based around "real" magic, i.e. not fantasy magic, and there are also a number of Wraeththu novellas and stories I've got half completed that I'd like to finish and bring out as a book. And I would dearly love to write a new novel. I've got so many ideas, notes and stray chapters I've written, but have so little time to get a good long run at anything. With full length works, I prefer not to have a lot of distractions that get in the way, but unfortunately with working on Immanion and its projects, my time tends to get eaten up.

DARRELL SCHWEITZER

Darrell Schweitzer is the author of about 300 short stories and the novels: *The White Isle*, *The Shattered Goddess* and *The Mask of the Sorcerer*. Along with George Scithers and John Betancourt, he refounded *Weird Tales* magazine in 1987 and continued to co-edit the magazine until 2007. He won a World Fantasy Award as co-editor of *Weird Tales*, along with Scithers.

Q: Over the past few years. We've seen a decline of short fiction markets that have legs. Do you see this as a decline in interest in short form fiction? How do you feel about the present state of the speculative short story?

A: Have we? Ralan.com and such places suggest there are more short fiction markets than ever. I can remember when there really *were* less than a dozen in the whole field. Today we have magazines, anthologies, paying (pro quality) websites like Card's *Medicine Show* or Tor.com, so I am not convinced the short fiction market is declining. I must also point out that Marvin Kaye and John Harlecher seem poised to revive *Weird Tales* and restore its weirdness.

Q: What do you think of today's speculative fiction with regards to the short story?

A: See above. I don't get to read as much of the current stuff as I would like. One's broader interests do get in the way. I confess the book I most recently finished was the world's oldest novel, *Callirhoe* by Chariton. Greek historical romance, written between about 25 BC to 50 AD. A genuine genre novel no less. No, I did not read it in Greek. I am afraid I shall have to revise my own claims. Romance, rather than fantasy is the oldest of prose genre forms. After that, I must turn to something more recent, a Tim Powers book I am reviewing for *Dead Reckonings*.

All I can say with confidence about the contemporary SF short story is that good stories are still being written and published, and no form is dead as long as it is still being produced. Ignore the doomsayers. The last time someone told me that SF had exhausted itself and could no longer be written, Cyberpunk happened the following year. If the field seems in the doldrums, it will renew itself.

Q: E-media (Internet and e-books): Friend or foe to the integrity of writing?

A: None of the above. If you read *Moby Dick* on a Kindle you are still reading *Moby Dick*. The internet may make piracy easier, which is another matter, but good writing is good writing and its integrity resides with the writer. In a publishing scene, I expect the mass-market paperback to disappear and be replaced by the e-book. But the hardcover, trade paperback, and paper magazine will continue to exist.

Q: What do you feel is the next step in speculative fiction?

A: See above. SF renews itself every few years. I think the new *Weird* has run its course and Steampunk may soon have difficulty keeping its pressure up, but something else will happen. We are always waiting for the Next Big Thing, confident that there will be one.

Q: Who are some of the more exciting up and coming authors you've seen lately?

A: Keep an eye out for John Fultz, Theodora Goss, and Holly Phillips. Also I very much enjoyed *The Postmortal* by Drew Magary, which is a Philip K. Dick Award finalist this year. I was one of the judges, but I cannot tell you what won until it is officially announced, or else I would be ritually strangled. (We judges are followed around by officially-appointed Thugees with scarves. I bet you didn't know that.) This relates back to my feelings about the state of the field. I was a PKD judge in the last year. I am really sick of steampunk zombie noir ... I notice that most of the really creative stuff these days is, like the Magary book, not actually being published with the science fiction label on it. Science Fiction has really gone mainstream, and hopefully this mainstream SF may feed some vigor back into the genre, which has way too many military SF or zombie series right now.

Q: What originally drew you to the dark side of fiction?

A: One for the very first adult level books I ever read or wanted to read (age 12) was *Dracula*. It's a natural affinity.

Q: What keeps you going in the writing gig? What excites you enough to motivate you?

A: Certainly it isn't making a living, because I have never done that with writing. What excites me is the act of creating a story good enough that I like it and have a pretty good idea that other people will like it too. As I have sold over 300 stories by now, I may be able to trust my judgment a little bit here.

Q: Vampires or zombies? Why?

A: I've written one real zombie story, "The Dead Kid," which is in *The Living Dead* (JJ Adams, ed) and a very small number of vampire stories. I am probably best known in that "field" for the two "Kvetchula" stories which may well be the best Jewish vampire stories written by a Gentile in the past several years. My (Jewish) mother-in-law, aged 82, read "Kvetchula's Daughter" and pronounced it "Funny as hell." "Why?" for whom? For me, when something starts to become a cliché I start getting silly. Certainly good vampire and zombie stories can still be written, but horror can be about something else. The best path may be back to basics. Vampires as evil. Zombies actually based on Haitian folklore rather than on George Romero movies.

Real vampires do not sparkle, of course.

Q: Will you be publishing an updated *Neil Gaiman Reader* or *The Thomas Ligotti Reader?*

A: I would like to update the Ligotti reader because by a ghastly accident a chapter which was supposed to be in the book isn't. But I don't know that the publisher is going to let me. The old edition just keeps on selling. If there is enough interest, I could always do a second volume. The Gaiman Reader, I am sorry to say, was not financially successful. I would need a new publisher. Wildside took a bit of a bath on that one. The irony is that for all Gaiman has a zillion times more fans than Ligotti, Ligotti criticism is a mature field, and I don't think Gaiman fans are really ready for lit-crit yet. The Gaiman equivalent of ST Joshi will write great articles when he is 40. Unfortunately, right now he is about 25.

Q: What led to your editing *The Secret History of Vampires?*

A: This is actually a good story. About the time *Alternate Kennedys* came out I started to joke that *Alternate Historical Vampire Cat Detectives* was only a matter of time. (I have written and published a story that would have fit into that book. Look up "The Adventure of the Hanoverian Vampires.") Anyway, at a party I started to kid one of the late lamented Marty Greenberg's assistants, "You know, alternate history sells and vampires sell, so how about Alternate Vampires, in which Elvis, Elizabeth Tudor, or whomever are vampires?" I thought I was joking. He thought I was pitching. He said, "Well, we're doing something like that already, but maybe in a year." Meanwhile, they came out with *Celebrity Vampires*. A year later the topic came up again—I had actually been called up about a Lloyd Biggle story because I am the agent for the Biggle estate—and before I knew it I had actually talked them into trying to sell the book, with the refinement that it was going to be Tim Powers style "secret history" rather than alternate history, with vampires. Then DAW went for it. I would be quite happy to do a second volume, if DAW is interested.

Q: How did *Tales from the Spaceport Bar* come to be?

A: This was George Scithers' idea. Ironically, neither of us ever hung out in bars much, or drank beyond a very minimal level. I still do not know what to order in a bar. It's a social skill I will probably (at age 59) never really learn. But there are a lot of good bar stories, and George knew that I could find some he hadn't thought of, so we collaborated on two volumes of them.

Q: Your interview collection *Speaking of Horror* had some heavy hitters in the genre. Who are some of the writers you'd have in a second volume?

A: I am going to have a second volume as soon as I can get the files assembled and turned in. Peter Straub, Gahan Wilson, Chet Williamson, Lisa Tuttle, Ramsey Campbell, Brian Lumley (again; the interview from HPL's Mag #3), Brian Hopkins, Sephira Giron, F. Paul Wilson . . . I have a rather long list to draw from. The irony is that I don't get to do horror interviews much anymore, as I do not seem to have a market for them. I still review SF writers and editors in every issue of Card's *Medicine Show*. I do not know if the new, revived *Weird Tales* will ever go in for interviews.

Q: What are you working on now? Anything to say to your fans?

A: I owe various people short stories. I am also working to scan, edit, and assemble a file of the companion stories to *The Shattered Goddess*, into a book called *Echoes of The Goddess*. These are dark/mythic fantasy stories set in the remote future. The Donning Co. was supposed to publish the book in the mid-'80s. Now I can get a Wildside/Borgo edition if I buckle down and assemble it. Alas, my scanning skills and software are such that scanning is scarcely better than retyping. All the stories predate my owning a computer. The good news is that but for an occasional clumsy phrase, I still like the stories.

If my agent can sell my young adult novel *The Dragon House*, I would like to write a sequel. But that has not happened yet. The sequel would be the world's first humorous (or somewhat humorous) Cthulhu Mythos novel for teens. Just what the world needs. My most recent sale was a story to Joe Pulver's *Grimescribe's Puppets*, a Thomas Ligotti tribute anthology. I am working on an anthology myself, about which I must be vague at this point because it is almost entirely invitational and I do not want to be deluged. I've also recently sold stories to volumes 2 and 3 of ST Joshi's *Black Wings* (of Cthulhu) series, and to the new *Weird Tales*. I wrote something for their Elder Gods issue, but they decided to use something else of mine in that issue, so the story I actually wrote for the occasion will appear later. The forces of the marketplace seem to be pushing me in a Cthulhuoid direction right now. A collection of my Cthulhu Mythos stories is inevitable as soon as I have enough available for reprinting to fill a book. Believe it or not, I have not spent years and years writing Lovecraft pastiches. I did no serious Mythos fiction until quite recently.

BRIAN HODGE

He's written an armful of novels or horror/crime, nonfiction that shows no signs of slowing, and about 100 short stories. He has seen numerous finalist slots for the Stoker, the World Fantasy Award, and the CWA Dagger Award, and obtaining the International Horror Guild Award for outstanding short fiction, *With Acknowledgments to Sun Tzu*.

Brian is online at: http://www.brianhodge.net and http://warriorpoetblog.com

Q: What is Horror's biggest asset: the scare, or the exploration of the darker topics of the human condition?

A: For my money, Column B, definitely. Exploring the human condition is the highest goal of any kind of storytelling. Or should be, most of the time. Not that you can't make room for something purely frivolous. But if all you're doing is conducting an exercise in stringing together a sequence of technical tricks to keep someone reading, without getting into your own deeper thoughts or feelings on anything, observations from your own life experience … that's not something I'd be much interested in reading. Or if I read it, it probably wouldn't strike me as in any way memorable.

That issue was at the heart of my all-time favorite piece of reader mail. I've never liked the term "fan mail," because I'd rather think of it as a lateral dialogue. But it was from a Florida prison convict. He'd been in for decades, I guess. He said he'd read 20,000 books in that time, and upon reading *Prototype*, it was the first time he'd ever felt compelled to contact the author. He wanted to tell me that my gifts were wasted on fiction and that I should turn to nonfiction philosophy, something like that.

How sweet is that? Saying, in essence, "You did this so well you shouldn't do it anymore." But of course, fiction is where those sorts of explorations come most alive for me.

Q: Spirituality in a variety of forms is a thread through several of your books. Why is that?

A: I'm afraid this one is going to follow a lot of tributaries. At the heart of it, your art or craft is invariably going to reflect your interests and obsessions. As well, for a lot longer than horror has had to make room for, say, slasher movies and the likes of *Saw* and *Hostel*, it's had a metaphysical component, with other realities and dimensions, so the spirit side is much older turf, and certainly more expansive.

But why the draw, on a personal level? It's just a fascinating realm to explore. There's no end to the tangents and permutations. It's like a Mandelbrot set: The closer you look, the more it unfolds. And, arguably, nothing has had more influence on shaping human history. Some might make a case for things like disease and technology, but to me, all that is vying for second. Although at this point you really have to start making a distinction between raw numinous experience, and the institutions and dogmas set up to corral and control and own it. You ask about exploring the darker side of the human condition? Ultimately, what's darker than these institutions and dogmas when they run amok? What's more terrifyingly relentless than people convinced their god is telling them to subjugate and kill? What's worse than the idea of some capricious force that toys with you for amusement, or regards you as less than you might regard an ant that meets your shoe sole?

Plus, I've always been relentlessly curious about what's on the other side of the veil, and the mechanisms of interactivity back and forth. I've had a number of intriguing experiences, some of which I've sought out and some of which have just happened, and most are personal enough that I'd rather keep them to myself, but here's one that's kind of delightful:

Before Doli and I could move to Colorado, we first had to sell her house, and it wasn't moving. It was on the market for the better part of two years. Then somebody gave her one of those St. Joseph statues from the gift shop of the local Catholic hospital. You know, those cheap plastic statues you bury in your yard, and it's supposed to prompt the sale of your home? Now, by this time, I'd already written stuff like "The Dripping of Sundered Wineskins," so, to put it lightly, it wasn't like I had a particularly reverent attitude about the whole thing. But the place sold within two or three weeks.

That's not even the really cool part. I have this friend, Denise, that I've known since junior high. We'd run into each other every so often, and she'd come to my earliest book signings, but overall, we're talking very infrequent, random encounters. Then one night I dreamed that she came to visit me in a jail cell, and let me out. Less than a week later, she showed up to look at the house, and bought it.

What's going on behind things like that? With the statue, sure, you can dismiss it as coincidence, but then, it's been a coincidence for a great many frustrated home sellers. You could think of it as a process-oriented equivalent of a tulpa—something that takes on an objective reality after the belief in it reaches a kind of critical mass. Or something like one of Rupert Sheldrake's morphic fields. And the dream, well, that's like a wink from the universe, which definitely seems to have a sense of humor sometimes.

I just try to stay open, and can't see the universe as a hostile place—quite the contrary —unless that's how you choose to relate to it, with hostility and fear as a kind of programming language. So when I'm in that mode as a writer, I guess what I'm really doing is just spinning cautionary tales: Be careful what you believe in, because you might get it, and in ways you don't expect.

Q: You're also a musician; what sort of music do you enjoy, and what would the first-time listener of your music be able to expect?

A: Well, musician may be pushing it. Sound deformer, that might be more like it.

I listen to a lot of ambient music, all sorts of sub-genres, because I find it easiest to work to. It's moody, it's atmospheric, but it's not intrusive or distracting. Beyond that, it gets pretty varied: classical and baroque, Nordic black metal, apocalyptic folk, gothic-industrial, Celtic, Tuvan, didgeridoo, soundtracks to sword movies, and the list goes on. Perennial favorites include Steve Roach, Fields of the Nephilim, Skinny Puppy, Nine Inch Nails, Courtney Love, Dimmu Borgir, Tom Waits, Gary Numan, Loreena McKennitt, Ordo Equitum Solis, Sol Invictus, Rush. Right now I'm on a Rammstein kick. Before that it was vintage Tangerine Dream.

As for my own efforts, again, I tend mostly toward the ambient direction, kind of soundtrackish at times. Painting with sound is a good way to describe a lot of it. Sometimes it has ties to my writing; sometimes not, and it's like doing aural landscapes.

Q: As a gearhead from the Eighties, I feel compelled to ask you about your rig, and how has it changed through the years?

A: Not surprisingly, it's become a lot more computer-centered. The earliest pieces I had were these analog castoffs you could pick up cheap after the first digital instruments emerged: a Moog Prodigy, an ARP Solina String Ensemble, a Yamaha CP-30 electronic piano. I sold all of those for nice profits when vintage analog gear started to enjoy a resurgence. A Memorymoog drifted through for a few years, too, then I sold that to a collector in Germany. It'd be cool to still have them—well, not so much the CP-30— but you can't keep everything.

With the early gear, I didn't have a way to record anything, until Roland came out with their VS line of digital multitrack recorders. Compact marvels at the time, but now, even those seem rudimentary compared to programs like Logic, which I run in an 8-core Mac Pro. Around the same time I got a VS-840 workstation, I got a Roland JP-8000, one of the first virtual analog synths — still have it, still love it — and since then, it's just built up from there, into that ridiculous gear list I have on my web site. I do still love the hardware synthesizers and modules, but now I mostly get things rolling with software synths and sample libraries. It's all just so seductively self-contained. The last two bits of hardware I've bought were USB MIDI controller keyboards: a Yamaha KX8—I'd been waiting years for Yamaha to put their piano action in a pure controller—and an Akai MPK49, which has an excellent control surface.

Q: Was there one particular moment when you decided to pursue an outlet in music?

A: Not really. I had lessons in clarinet and piano when I was a kid, and more piano in college. It's just something that's always been there, to one degree or another. What triggered its current degree was when my novel *Wild Horses* sold at auction. I had this nice fat influx of cash, and decided to hit the reset button on my gear set-up. I have this saying that came out of that: "Success in one field of creative endeavor should fund the ongoing abuse of another."

The only definitive moment was when I took up the didgeridoo. The first Steve Roach album I heard was *Australia: Sound of the Earth*, which features an aboriginal didge player named David Hudson. He is to the didge what Eddie Van Halen is to the guitar. Hearing that, my reaction was like, "I have GOT to make this sound!"

Q: What makes your expansion of the Horror genre as you see it attract the fanbase you have?

A: I can only echo feedback I've gotten from readers and reviewers and editors. Probably the first thing comes down to characters, the work I put into trying to make them as real and compelling and three-dimensional as I can. And that there's a definite emotional connection to them, and what happens to them. Also, that I try to avoid the obvious, the predictable. That I usually strive to be writing *about* something, not solely escapism that's only operating on the surface. For some readers, at least, that I've never stopped working to refine my prose style into something that's smooth and effortless, sometimes rhythmic and lyrical. None of which has anything to do with horror per se. It's all to do with the craft of writing, period.

Q: What led to the writing of *Wild Horses*? It was quite a departure from what readers had, up until that point, had been expecting from you.

A: That came after the years I spent under the Dell/Abyss imprint, where I'd done four novels, each one grimmer than the last, culminating with *Prototype*. As weird as it may sound, I hadn't learned, at that point, to protect myself from my own material, the places I was going emotionally to do the work. It was like the writing equivalent of method acting, where you *become* the role. It was taking a real toll, and *Prototype* was the nadir of that. I've seen and heard all kinds of assessments about *Prototype* in that regard. Writer Edward Lee called it the most depressing novel he'd ever read, if also the most illuminating, for that reason. My editor on it, Jeanne Cavelos, called it unbearable. Someone else, the novel *not* to read if you're feeling suicidal. More recently, one of my physical instructors said that, in terms of bleakness in everything he's read, it runs second only to Cormac McCarthy's *The Road*. It's not just me reacting that way.

So I came out of *Prototype* with two problems. I had to do something different for my own well-being. And even if that weren't a factor, it still felt like if I tried to go any deeper, it was going to turn into self-parody. The only option was to ricochet in another direction entirely… something that also appealed just for a change of pace. Fortunately, I'd done this longish crime piece called "Miles To Go Before I Weep," which at the time was unpublished, because the book it was supposed to go into fell apart, as did the second one. It was the core of Allison and Tom's story, and I realized I wasn't ready to turn loose of these characters yet, and that there were more waiting under the surface. So that was the road that beckoned, and grew into *Wild Horses*.

Q: Your novel, *On Earth As It Is in Hell*, takes place in the Hellboy canon. Had you been a fan of the comics or movies? Were you envisioning either medium when writing?

A: By then I was a fan, yeah. The roots of this go back a few years earlier, when Dark Horse Comics did an anthology of Hellboy short stories, called *Odd Jobs*. The editor, Christopher Golden, invited me to do something for it, and at that time, no, I wasn't familiar with the character beyond seeing the covers in comic shops. They sent me some stuff, and it clicked with me, so despite the crash course, I thought I could do it justice.

In a situation like this, where I get asked to play with somebody else's toys, I look for overlaps in interest. It was obvious that Mike Mignola, Hellboy's creator, has an interest in folklore of the British Isles and Europe, and that was something I could tap into, so I did a story called "Far Flew the Boast of Him," which is a phrase from *Beowulf*. At least from the translation I reread to do the story, which has Hellboy encountering a reincarnated Grendel after he's slaughtered a group of medievalist battle reenactors.

A few years later, come to find out, that story is one of Mike's favorites among other people's uses of his character. Apparently he felt I really got the feel and flavor of things. The success of that first Hellboy movie led to Mike setting up a deal with Simon & Schuster to license the rights to four novels, and of course they needed people to write them. On the basis of that story, I was on the short list. The novels were rooted in Mike's own version of his universe, rather than the film version—there *are* differences—so that's what I was staying true to.

Q: *Prototype* may very well be one of the best examples of what could be referred to as 'Thinking man's Horror.' Would this be an accurate statement from your point-of-view?

A: That's such a nice compliment, I could hardly be so rude as to disagree, now could I? Yeah, I'd hoped it would be food for thought, and the fact that there's nothing supernatural about it, that it involves a chromosomal mutation and some rather Jungian concepts, maybe that helps.

Q: How did you get involved with the mosaic storytelling in *Zombie Apocalypse! Fightback*? Can you tell us what the story will be about?

A: These books are the brainchildren of editor Stephen Jones, and they straddle a weird line between novel and anthology. Steve's approach has been to conceptualize each book's direction, and the individual segments that make up the whole, then match each segment to the writer he feels will open it up and bring a unique strength to it.

The section he wanted me for focuses on sport fighting with the living dead. Or as I think of it, the UFC with zombies. Steve knew that I have an interest in combat sports, and some knowledge there, and some experience with the training and sparring, so that made me the go-to guy.

That was my main contribution to the book, but I also did a shorter piece that helps recap the origin material from the first book, from a different angle. This one was an improvisation, almost, after I sent Steve an article about a medieval plague pit excavation going on in London that dovetailed with what he'd already conceived. It was funny—here I am in Colorado, reading the *New York Times*, sending Steve news on an archaeological dig in his own city, which he wasn't aware of. I'd only thought he might file it away for possible future reference with the third book, but he came right back with another commission: adapt it, run with it. It worked out well, too. He says it fits in perfectly.

Q: What can we expect from *Without Purpose, Without Pity*?

A: It's a good-sized novella, the longest thing I've done that doesn't break the usual word-length finish line that constitutes a full novel. It's set in the near future, to give enough time for the real-life aspects of the core premise to play out to their worst-case-scenario conclusion: that Las Vegas is an unsustainable city because of its escalating water needs relative to the dwindling available supply. Just yesterday I saw an article on how the Nevada state government has approved a plan for Vegas to begin pumping in groundwater from rural areas 300 miles away, at a cost of between $3- and $15 billion. You have to love that fivefold margin of error. So the ranchers and Indian tribes get screwed, of course, but on the bright side, one of things making out great would be, and I quote, "a new, golf-course-based city in Coyote Spring Valley in the Mojave Desert."

Where's a good, low-level asteroid strike when you really need one?

I digress. The novella: It's an odd mix of elements. This future dystopian aspect, but there's also this Lovecraftian element that's asserted itself after the socio-economic and environmental collapse. And it's told through the world of boxers, in particular what's going on with a former heavyweight contender whose limbs have started to mutate. Plus, as a bonus, it has the weirdest Thai rope fight ever conceived.

Q: What inspired you to write "With Acknowledgments To Sun Tzu" from your collection, *Picking The Bones*?

A: I originally wrote that for an anthology themed around art and artists. After the invitation to contribute came along, I went through my usual contrarian thought process. That is, when there's a unifying theme, there's also usually an obvious direction to go in, and I try to avoid it like the Ebola virus. This tactic has always served me well. In this instance it meant throwing out the usual notions of art and artists and the like. Then I got to reflecting on the title of the Sun Tzu classic, *The Art of War*. OK, what if you took *that* to mean a medium of expression? Not long before, I'd watched a documentary on combat photographers, and it's such an outlier culture, you know—they're running into places that every other civilian is trying to run away from—so to me that automatically made for an interesting dynamic. Plus I've done a number of works in which whatever terrible things may be going on the surface reality, they're still just ripples above these vast, powerful currents flowing underneath, and this fit right into that, as well.

Q: In your bio, you talk about how when you were young, you would scribble on bits of wood and attach them to trees, 'Apparently trying to communicate something to whoever might come along later.' What would you have done if whatever or whoever had come to discuss this with you as a boy and/or as an adult?

A: That's a good question! I never thought of that. I mean, when I wrote that line I was thinking of it in mundane terms, but the way you're asking it makes it sound more mysterious, more esoteric. Which is just as valid. Who knows what was going through my head at the time, what I thought I had to say before I even knew the alphabet? And who's to say that some sort of contact hasn't happened, and I didn't recognize it for what it was? There *is* the other anecdote I paired that with, about the bullets, and that retroactive sense of somehow being guarded, being protected from my own childish ignorance. Maybe that's how these things work: with great subtlety.

Q: You're a practitioner of Krav Maga; what made you pursue that particular form of self-defense?

A: We might need to define that a little more, for clarity's sake. Krav Maga is the hand-to-hand combat system of the Israeli Defense Forces. I'm in my fifth year of it, and when I started, I was looking for a different way to work out. I was bored with years of running and looking for new ways to lift the same weights. I'd seen the sign for this place, and my friend Nickolas Cook had taken up Krav several months before in Arizona, and spoke highly of it, so I went for a sample class. I spent the first 20 minutes wondering what I'd gotten myself into, but by the end of the hour I was laying down ink for a year.

My thinking at first was like three birds, one stone: I'd get great workouts, with zero chance of boredom, *and* be picking up a valuable skill set, *and* it might expose me to material I could use in writing. All true. But it's gone a lot deeper than that. When you stay with something like this long enough, committing to it and internalizing the subtler aspects and tenets, I fully believe it can make you a better person, in a lot of ways.

I appreciate the background of it. The early foundations of Krav were laid down in Eastern Europe in the 1930s, by a man named Imi Lichtenfeld. He wanted a way to equip his community with a direct, effective means to deal with attacks by Nazi thugs. As such, it's not strictly a martial art, but a system that draws from a variety of traditions—boxing, kickboxing, Muay Thai, Brazilian Jiu Jitsu, escrima, military weapons applications, etc.—and even now it continues to evolve and refine, so I like that fluidity. And where I train, the lineage is very direct. Imi introduced it to the U.S. in the 1980s through a guy named Darren Levine, who was the chief instructor for the owner of my school, James Hiromasa, who's an internationally renowned instructor in his own right.

Plus it's full of great people, instructors and fellow students alike. In my years with it, I've never seen anyone come to it with a bad, or bad*ass*, attitude. Not once. People seem to get the humility aspect of it right away, and maybe a little later, the service aspect, the guardian aspect. I did some more advanced training with several specialists a few weeks ago, and one of them, his metaphor for us is sheepdogs: pack animals with a high regard for the safety and well-being of others.

Q: What is next for you?

A: There's quite a lot in the works. We've already covered *Without Purpose, Without Pity*, which is just now becoming available in early digital format, with the hardcover edition coming in a couple months.

I'm putting together my fifth collection of short fiction, called *No Law Left Unbroken*, which rounds up my crime-oriented shorter work, along with some new stuff. We're experimenting with this one as a digital-only release, with print-on-demand, I think. I'm also past the midway point of converting my backlist books over to e-book formats. That process is going smoothly now.

Cemetery Dance is doing a big fat hardcover edition of my early post-apocalyptic novel *Dark Advent*. I did an extensive polish of that one, to the extent that it's a brand new draft. Not a different novel, but it was such early work that I really wanted to take the opportunity to make the immaturities of execution grow up a little.

Distinct from that, but related, CD is also planning a special end-of-the-world issue of the magazine, in which various authors who've wiped out the world already contribute do it again, in shorter form. There are a couple-three other short fiction appearances on the horizons, as well.

And, finally, there's the novel-in-progress, that's been taking way too reprehensibly long. It's already longer than eight of my previous ten novels, and should easily surpass *Dark Advent* and *Deathgrip* by the time it's done. Most writers seem to have one of these at some point: the one that turns into your Mount Everest, your Tour de France. It's yet another departure, which has been a big part of the challenge.

PAUL DI FILIPPO

Paul Di Filippo has behind him hundreds of short stories, some of which are to be found in *The Steampunk Trilogy*, *Ribofun*, and *Lost Page* and his novella, *A Year in the Linear City*, was nominated for multiple awards. Another collection, *Destroy All Brains*, is a rare treasure. And if you can find it, do yourself a favor and buy it!

You can find Paul at http://paul-di-filippo.com

Q: What led to the writing of "Waves" and "Smart Magma?"

A: This story is actually the second in a highly abbreviated series. And both pieces were commissioned by wonderful editors, so they deserve a lot of the inspirational credit. First, Lou Anders was putting together an anthology titled *Live Without a Net*, the premise for which was worlds and futures with non-computer-based internets. I came up with a piece titled "Clouds and Cold Fires," in which computing power was distributed literally across the skies, embedded in meteorological phenomena. Moreover, those computational powers were Singularity-powerful. Additionally, most of humanity had gone post-human, leaving Earth to uplifted animals and the dregs of our species. Having written one adventure in this venue, I had a few years pass until Mike Ashley asked for a contribution to *THE MAMMOTH BOOK OF MINDBLOWING SF*, one of several original stories in a reprint book. I had implied further adventures for a new generation of characters in "Clouds," and also felt there was more in this venue to explore, so it was off to the races!

Q: With works like *Wikiworld*, how do you combine a bit of satire with good old-fashioned humor?

A: Humor is always better if it has a bite, and satire often provides the fangs. The baseline human situation is always pretty absurd--our bodily limitations, our emotions, our aspirations, our vices--but if you can add in something topical and give it an unexpected surreal twist, then you often have a powerful combination. So my recipe is to find something topical and see what kinds of comic characters best match the theme.

Q: You've done quite a bit of e-publishing. With the ability for writers can have now to present their work for all to see, do you see any liabilities of electronic media v. traditional print?

A: I actually consider myself behind the curve with e-books. Out of my roughly thirty print volumes, only about one is available electronically *(Cosmocopia)* as well as a smattering of shorter works. I'm very happy to offer my work on any platform that appeals to readers. But personally, I still prefer hardcopy for my own pleasures. Having said that, I should also announce that Richard Curtis is working to port almost all my short fiction over to his E-reads venue. So stay tuned!
http://neconebooks.com/byauthor.htm

As for liabilities versus advantages for readers and authors both, I think the latter outweigh the former, so long as we can sustain a technological civilization. But if bad times come, my bet is on paper!

Q: *Fuzzy Dice* is (at least) eclectic storytelling. How did you manage to work through 144 Chapters with a story that changes approach and style in a cavalier way?

A: My role model here, as I've said publicly before, was A. E. van Vogt with his famous writing advice to "do something new every 750 words." I always loved van Vogt's stuff and wondered if I could emulate him. Of course, infamous idiot savants like Harry Stephen Keeler often did the same thing, with charmingly disastrous results. Hopefully, I came across more like van Vogt than like Keeler! It was a challenge, but actually proved liberating and fun, trying to warp the plot every thousand words or so, and come up with zillions of neat ideas. Can't do it every outing like AEVV did, but once was a blast.

Q: How does your admiration of Thomas Pynchon affect your work? Do others see Pynchon-esque touches in your work you didn't know were there?

A: I truly believe that in 100 years, Pynchon will be seen as the Dickens of the 20th and 21st centuries. Not in the sense that he embodied the same writerly flavors as Dickens, but in the sense that both men were utterly emblematic of the zeitgeist and tapped directly into the strongest currents. Having this admiration and estimation of him, I have naturally sought to try to incorporate some of the things he does, in search of similar effects. So I can point out to you deliberate pastiches of mine, like "Karuna, Inc.," which is modeled on *The Crying of Lot 49*. But undoubtedly, since he's shaped my worldview so strongly (I first encountered him in college forty years ago, when my favorite English professor offered extra credit for reading *Gravity's Rainbow*), there are lots of unconscious emulations of him in my work as well. Heck, just the silly character names alone are rampant!

Q: Which five books would you want if you were to be stranded on an island?

A: That's a tough one! Here goes, anyhow
Walden
Leaves of Grass
Gravity's Rainbow
Dhalgren
Little, Big

Q: You've said, "I am always threatening to write my great 'horsepower SF' novel starring Bishop Berkeley, The Philosopher's Star. Please be patient." How much closer has that come to being a reality?

A: Do you know the distance from here to the Oort Cloud? I'm now somewhat beyond the orbit of our Moon on my way to that distant destination.

Q: You've referred to yourself as a "Willy-nilly Buddhist." Can you define the beliefs of the aforementioned Buddhist?

A: Well, my personal Buddhism evolved this way. I read scores of books on Buddhism. Then I practiced at a Buddhist temple for several years. Then I threw everything away except "Be kind!"

Q: *Ciphers* contains a great deal of Buddhist lore. Are all of your works united by the thread of your beliefs in some way?

A: I try not to let any one particular lens or filter color my writings, but of course it's almost impossible to separate one's ideology and morality and ethics and biases from the process of fiction creation. Still, I like to think that I can inhabit mindsets and worldviews that are totally alien or antithetical to my personal preferences and write fiction from that viewpoint. Isn't such selfless empathy part of the writer's essential kit?

Q: *Ciphers* also starts out with the words "Am I live, or am I Memorex." Do you feel that not only noting a catch phrase, but a particular manufacturer hurts the legs a given story may have with a sort of pop-culture reference?

A: That's a tough line to walk. *Ciphers* is indeed overstuffed with very transient allusions that may well be impenetrable to new generations of readers. But you always hope the underlying attractions of the tale allow such readers to blip over what they don't get, or even motivates them to do research. I watch tons of old movies from the 1930s and 1940s and there is often dialogue that references outdated cultural touchstones. But generally, my appreciation of a well-constructed and well-acted film is not ruined by such minor hurdles.

Q: *Ciphers* is a "Rock and Roll Mystery." With that in mind, what kind of Rock music do you like to listen to?

A: My mate Deborah and I have a goal of listening together to one new CD every day, and I try to keep the playlist very eclectic. One day might be Angelique Kidjo, followed by Frank Sinatra, then Foster the People, then Charles Mingus, then Coldplay, then Springsteen, then Richard Bona, then Gregg Allman...and so forth. Old to new, rock to jazz, pop to American Songbook. About the only thing I can't groove to is hip hop. Just got a tin ear for that genre.

Q: Has your SF writing caused any sort of inner conflict with yourself in light of Buddhism?

A: Not so far! Buddhism offers a big spectrum of role models. So long as I keep Ikkyu in mind, I can't go too far wrong. http://en.wikipedia.org/wiki/Ikkyu

Q: What are you working on now?

A: Literally this moment, I have to start a steampunk story to accompany my GOH appearance in Italy at Italcon 2012. It will be set in Venice and titled *A Palazzo in the Stars*. After that, I hope to get a novel off the ground. It's been too long since I've worked at those lengths.

Q: What do you see on the horizon for the SF genre?

A: Damien Broderick and I wrote a book that is due out soon, titled *Science Fiction: The 101 Best Novels 1985-2010*. Doing that survey showed me the immense accomplishments of the past few decades and made me confident that the genre will continue to perform superbly. As for specific trends, it's hard to say. Ernest Cline's *Ready Player One* seemed to me to represent a new type of SF, savvy about gaming culture and the internet in a new way that some older works aren't. Maybe we're just starting to get some new "voices under 30" that will do amazing and unprecedented things.

Q: Anything you'd like to tell your readers they may not already know about you?

A: I make a mean dish of carbonara! The secret is parsley.

STEVE RASNIC TEM

Steve's short fiction has been compared to the work of Franz Kafka, Dino Buzzati, Ray Bradbury, and Raymond Carver, but to quote Joe R. Lansdale: "Steve Rasnic Tem is a school of writing unto himself." His 300 plus published pieces have garnered him a British Fantasy Award and nominations for the World Fantasy and Bram Stoker Awards.

You can find Steve's blog here: http://www.m-s-tem.com/tems/blog1.php/home

Q: Do you feel that the simple tag of "Horror" applies to your work?

A: "Horror" is a rather broad brush, and not a very useful description except when applied to certain short stories which have an obsessive, singularly emotional sort of effect. As a label it becomes particularly problematic when applied to the novel, because some greater context is required or the horror has no meaning--in fact it may seem a bit silly. At the longer lengths I think we need to know what is being risked, what is it that may be lost. The whole of human experience needs to come into play—at least if it's going to be a good novel. When we look at it in those terms "horror" becomes but one aspect of a writer's body of work. I think that applies to most writers—not just me.

Q: When did you start pursuing writing as a serious career move?

A: I'd graduated from VPI in Blacksburg with a bachelor's in English Education. Not a terribly useful degree since I'd decided I didn't want to teach. I'd always wanted to be a writer, so I decided to find out if I could become one. I had no idea how to do that, so I applied to various graduate programs in Creative Writing, just to see what would happen. I was accepted into a few, but Bill Tremblay, a poet at Colorado State University, decided I was some sort of "southern surrealist" and wanted me in his program, so I went out there. That was my first step toward writing as a career, back in 1975.

Q: What sort of reading matter did you have around the house when you were growing up?

A: Very little. I'd bought comics with my allowance, but the only books we had around the house for a long time were a bible and some *Reader's Digest* condensed books which seemed to accumulate like randomly acquired house decorations, but which no one ever read. Almost no one in our small Appalachian farming community had any appreciable number of books. My grandfather was an exception, having inherited a couple of hundred dusty volumes from my great-grandfather--including some ghost stories. There was also a few hundred "trashy" crime and western paperbacks stored in wooden crates that belonged to a cousin. I read those when I visited--even though they were off-limits.

At some point my mother talked my dad into getting a set of encyclopedias, but I was primarily interested in the set of children's classics that came with them—*Robin Hood, the Tales of King Arthur, Huck Finn, Sherlock Holmes*. I read those volumes multiple times.

Q: What makes Horror fans pursue the dark side of storytelling?

A: Horror fans like dark fiction for a variety of reasons, depending on age and experience. Some people simply enjoy being scared; for others it fulfills a spiritual need. I'm sure for some younger readers it's just the notion of being contrary to everything ordinary people consider good and heroic—it's yet another way to piss off their parents. Some find it therapeutic. I think for a lot of people horror entertainment is a rehearsal for tragedy—both tragedies past and tragedies to come. One of the interesting aspects of that dynamic is that some readers prefer horror whose specific circumstances remind them of their own. For others that's the last thing they want—they're seeking to escape those troubles. Horror provides them with a safe place to deal with those materials.

Q: What sort of things would we see as a fly on the wall when you collaborate with your wife Melanie?

A: It would be like watching paint dry I'm afraid. We'll talk about a project in general at first—at dinner or during some lull, and then the rest is just passing the story back and forth via email, rewriting each other and advancing the story incrementally until it's done. A lot of improvisation goes on. And compromise.

Q: *Daughters*, co-written with Melanie, is a delightfully written story which deals with the loss of magic and the rise of technology. Is the book a parable reflecting our own modern world?

A: Ah, *Daughters!* It was great fun to do, but it's a book of ours very few have ever read. At least we have it available as an ebook now. Yes, it's very much in parable mode, but it's as much about psychological states and human development as it is about modern culture. I think human beings start out with a whole lot of magic in their heads, which is gradually pushed out as they use technology. But the imagination—which for me is another way of saying "magic"—is essential, I think, to becoming a well-rounded human being. But you have to make this journey from the superstitious to the creative. The key is finding a way to allow logic and the imagination to co-exist.

Q: What is your opinion on the state of Speculative Fiction these days?

A: I think there are more fine writers working in the field today than ever before, and they come from a range of backgrounds. This means a variety of styles and approaches and ways of viewing the world. We're seeing more and more writers from overseas and from other cultures. And we're seeing more writers who actually know how to write fiction, as opposed to writers with great ideas but whose prose is stilted and whose characters are cardboard.

Q: What other art form would you like to pursue?

A: I love to draw and paint. I make no claims for my talents in that arena, but it's something I enjoy doing.

Q: What inspired *Deadfall Hotel?*

A: I've always loved stories concerning haunted architecture, and I'm fascinated by buildings in general—the infrastructure, the electrical and plumbing systems, how they're maintained, how variations in space and color and lighting and furnishing can affect us emotionally, how we can make those spaces our own. The whole psychology of the house and how these structures evolve as substitutes for/elaborations on the womb, and the greater sense of a "body" we all live inside.

All this went into *Deadfall.* I wanted, in a sense, to write about the ultimate haunted hotel, which could also serve as a metaphor for horror fiction in general. I wanted to create a vessel which could contain as much of this as possible.

Q: *Among the Living* strikes me as a great example of economy of storytelling without sacrificing the texture of the story or characters. What influenced you most in this type of writing?

A: The novelette and the novella are the perfect lengths for horror fiction, I think. They're short enough that they can sustain a certain obsessive focus and intensity. And yet they're long enough that you can explore various aspects of the same idea, ring complications on those ideas, and develop your characters more fully than you might in a short story. Too often the additional length of the horror novel makes that obsessional quality seem strained. And in the novella/novelette the length of the piece forces you to use a pretty tight, predetermined structure, which helps avoid that "sagging middle" syndrome you so often get in the novel.

Q: *The Book of Days* took an interesting tack in storytelling in that each day, a man tries to resolve his own sanity. What was the inspiration for the subject matter and format of storytelling?

A: The format was driven by the circumstances of the writing. I wrote the first draft on the old GENIE online bulletin board system. There was a section of the board set aside for professional genre writers, and Bruce Holland Rogers started this "Steve Rasnic Tem" discussion topic. So he gave me this venue, and I wanted to make use of it, preferably daily so people would have a reason to visit it. And I wanted it to be something creative.

So I needed to come up with a project that had more-or-less logical small daily units, which could be improvised in the composition. Improvisation seemed important because of the time constraints, and because I was seriously interested in improvisational working methods at the time (I still am). So I thought of a diary format, and to spark the improvisations I thought of these "This Day in History" snippets you could find on calendars and in daily newspapers.

Finally I tried to think about what kind of person would feel compelled to write such diary entries. The novel naturally evolved from there.

Q: A bulk of your work revolves around normal people in decidedly abnormal situations. Do you feel that's an accurate observation?

A: More or less—that's the standard circumstance, certainly, for most genre fiction. The only way I might refine that description is that I think my characters tend to discover during the course of the story that the abnormality, in fact, is in them, and that "normalcy" is a bit of an illusion.

Q: Are there any authors new to the scene who scare you?

A: Scare me? Well, a lot scares me. But the newer writers who really interest me include the Simon's—Unsworth, Bestwick, and Stranzas—and writers like Gary McMahon, Laird Barron, John Langan, Catherine Valente. But there are SO many.

Q: What are you working on currently?

A: I have a science fiction novel in progress—*Before Oblivion*, a couple of YAs, an expansion of my "zombie" story *Bodies & Heads* into a novel, a number of other things.

Q: Any last words?

A: But if I reveal them now, they wouldn't really be my last words, now would they?

NORMAN PRENTISS

Norman walked away with a Stoker for Superior Achievement in Short Fiction for "In the Porches of My Ears." His first novel, *Invisible Fences*, was published by Cemetery Dance and his short prose has been seen in *Tales From the Gorezone*, and *The Year's Best Dark Fantasy and Horror*, among many other collections and anthologies. His essays on Gothic and sensation literature have appeared in *Colby Quarterly* and *The Thomas Hardy Review*.

Norman's little piece of Cyberspace is: normanprentiss.com

Q: You've been referred to as one of the genre's rising stars. Does that get in your head in a negative way?

A: It's an incredibly flattering thing to hear, especially in light of how much respect I have for other writers described with similar words. As far as anything negative: maybe it's a tough label to live up to, putting a bit of pressure on? I don't really think of it that way, though. I'm mostly trying to live up to my previous book or story, to write something I'm proud to put my name on. That's where the real pressure comes, for me.

Q: Having won two Bram Stoker Awards, does that have an effect on the process of your writing?

A: Not really—not in any direct way, at least. The one thing that has happened is that I've been invited to submit work to different markets. That hadn't happened before, so I'm sure the Stokers played a part there (in addition to my appearance in Ellen Datlow's and Paula Guran's Year's Best anthologies). When you're invited to submit, there's definitely a different kind of process: you really are thinking about where a story is going to *go*, and the invite itself might influence the story you write. A good example would be one I wrote for the recent Zombie vs. Robots anthology, *This Means War!*, a gig I owe to Paula Guran for recommending me to the editor. I'd never done a zombie *or* a robot story, so the great thing about the project is that it inspired me to do something new. Plus, Jeff Connor at IDW, the book's editor, was so generous with incredible, detailed feedback, and that helped me take the story to new levels. I love how the story came out, but I never would have written it—or even known how much I'd *want* to write it—without being asked.

Q: With "Four Legs in the Morning," did the story or monster come first?

I'm going to say the character of Dr. Sibley came first, then the title—and the story and the monster kind of followed from there. I'll leave it at that, to avoid spoilers!

Q: Will we be seeing any more of Dr. Sibley?

A: Definitely. Although, part of the idea is that you don't actually *see* Sibley that much. He's in the background, at the periphery of his own stories. The one I'm working on now is called "The Future of Literary Criticism," and it's a kind of origin story—Sibley's early years, when he's on the academic job market.

Q: Childhood trauma and the effects it has on adults as they mature in *Invisible Fences*. What was the reason you picked up that kind of narrative thread?

A: The novella grew out of a poem I'd written many years before, where I explored the idea of life-events staying with you as you try to go on with your life. For *Invisible Fences*, I thought in the back of my mind about the horror movie cliché where a family moves into a house, and learn that it's haunted. In that scenario, the ghost is a stranger, and the family's main crime is that they've made a bad real estate decision. For me, it's not as scary to be in a house haunted by somebody else's ghosts. They need to be *your* ghosts to be really scary.

Q: What led to the decision of your using older characters in your work?

A: I hadn't actually thought about this, so that's a good question! Maybe it has to do with my own age? I'd rather attribute it to my temperament, and my sense of what types of story I want to tell. Older characters have a wealth of life experiences to haunt them, and they collect more things to worry about over the years. But I like how scary and strange the world can be for children, too, and have done a lot from that perspective (including the first half of *Invisible Fences*).

Q: Has the Internet reduced the attention span of the modern reader?

A: Yes.

People said the same thing about MTV and movie editing. Pace, in print or film, is one of my most important criteria—at the same time, I like a story that builds, so some things I like might seem slow for some readers or viewers. That's what critics call "a deliberate pace," when they're being generous. If the work has atmosphere, or a fascinating tone, that keeps me interested.

Q: "In the Porches of My Ears" was not only a Bram Stoker winner, but a story with a great deal of heart some may not expect. What led to the writing of it?

A: Some friends of mine had a movie-going experience of sitting behind a narrating couple, and I latched onto that idea. What I looked at my story ideas, I realized that I often take something from life and make it worse. That's what horror writers do. That's what pessimists do, also, but there you go.

Q: Can you tell us about the status of your long-awaited novel-length work?

A: I've got several in the works, but the one I'm aiming to finish first should be completed this summer. There's a story called "Beneath Their Shoulders" that would be a kind of sneak-peek of the longer work: that story will be in an upcoming anthology from PS Publishing.

Q: What's on the horizon for you, Norman?

A: More stories here and there, including the *Shocklines* anthology from Cemetery Dance, and a Halloween story for another upcoming anthology. I'm doing a mini-collection of children-in-danger stories (3 reprints and 3 or so originals), called *The Book of Baby Names*—probably an ebook. And I'm really excited about an upcoming novella from Delirium called *The Fleshless Man*—that's set to be announced in July, with a print date of September. I've gotten some incredible early feedback about this book, and I can't wait for more people to get a chance to read it!

CHET WILLIAMSON

Since 1981, Chet has published twenty-five books and over a hundred short stories in anthologies and magazines as diverse as *The New Yorker*, *Playboy*, and *The Magazine of Fantasy and Science Fiction*. He is a playwright as well as an author and actor. That's his voice reading the audio versions of the works of Michael Moorcock, Tom Picirilli, and many others.

Find out more at: chetwilliamson.com

Q: What led to your acting in Joe Lansdale's *Christmas with the Dead?*

A: Joe called me and asked me if I'd be interested in doing a small but really good part in a film that he was producing. It was a crazed preacher, a cult leader really, who, in a post-zombie-apocalyptic world, gives Holy Communion to zombies by feeding them real flesh and blood. Sounded like something I'd love to do, so I sent Joe a video of me doing one of the scenes so that he and the director, Terrill Lee Lankford, could see it. They liked it enough for me to fly down to Nacogdoches, Texas, where the film was going to be shot, and spend two days reading with Lee and learning the basics of film acting. Though I've done a lot of stage acting (I've been a member of Actors' Equity for decades), I'd never done a feature film. Lee taught me more in an hour than I'd have learned in years of acting school. He just cut right to the chase, and I got what he was saying. The film was based on Joe's short story, and his son Keith wrote the screenplay. His daughter Kasey plays Ella, and his son-in-law, Adam Coats, plays the goofy neighbor Ray, so it's a real family affair. Joe's wife Karen even co-produced. It sounds like a back yard film, but it isn't. Lee got fully professional performances out of some people who'd never acted before, as well as some who were experienced film actors, and the film turned out great. It's funny, but also creepy and touching, and the characters really have that Lansdale charm. I've been to a few public showings, one at NECON, a small horror con, and audiences seem to really love it. I only shot for a week—in 110-degree weather in an East Texas July!—and I tore a blood vessel behind my larynx while I was screaming during the scene where I'm getting...um, chowed down on. Had to have a little surgery to fix it, but I'm finally back to normal. The whole experience was worth it, though!

Q: I'm a big fan of *The Final Verse*. Was there anything in particular that inspired the story?

A: I've always been a fan of roots music, like The Carter Family, Jimmie Rodgers, Bill Monroe, and other bluegrass and early country music. My son Colin moved from classical violin to bluegrass fiddle when he was in junior high, and I used to accompany him on guitar in fiddle contests (he won a lot of them). I've always liked Celtic music too, and played for about seven years in a Celtic duo called Fire in the Glen (CDs still available at the website!). But what really triggered the story was when Tom Monteleone asked me to do a recording of one of my stories for Borderlands Press. It would have been a CD/chapbook combo, and I thought about doing an original story rather than using a reprint, something I could write to be heard rather than just read. So I came up with the story idea, and then wrote an actual song, both lyrics and music, that was integrated into the story. I recorded it in Tom's home studio, but about then the economy took a bad turn and Tom had to cancel some projects and gave me back the story. I sent it to Gordon Van Gelder at *The Magazine of Fantasy and Science Fiction*, and he bought it for the magazine. Ellen Datlow then picked it for her *Best Horror of the Year* volume, so its readership turned out to be much greater than it might have been originally. I still plan to rerecord it at some point.

Q: Tell us a bit about your acting career?

A: I feel like I've acted since forever. I did tons in high school and college, got my Equity card in my twenties, and did primarily business theatre and summer stock. Then I started writing as a result of the business theatre, and gave up acting for nearly thirty years. In 1986 I got involved in a playwriting group, primarily just to work with people again, since writing is such a lonely occupation, and did a few readings. On the basis of that, people told me I should audition and act again, so I reactivated my union card and got some great gigs at some local theatres that use Equity actors. I've done Bottom in *A Midsummer Night's Dream*, Dylan Thomas in *A Child's Christmas in Wales*, and if the pieces fall into place, it looks like a performing arts group I currently chair, Creative Works of Lancaster, will be doing *The Woman in Black*, in which I'll do one of the only two roles. I've also used my acting chops to narrate audiobooks for Crossroad Press. I've recorded a number of my own works, but also novels by Michael Moorcock, Tom Piccirilli, David Niall Wilson, Irving Wallace, John Skipp and Craig Spector, Zoe Winters, and others. I recently finished doing Joe Lansdale's *The Magic Wagon* and Neal Barrett Jr.'s *The Hereafter Gang*. All are available at audible.com

Q: What makes an actor want to pursue the considerably more solitary role of writer?

A: The ironic thing is that I went into writing because I thought it was a more stable profession than acting. The more fool I! And of course, with writing you can play all the roles in your story. You become the director, the writer, costume and set designers, and all the actors. That's a pretty heady assignment for a former actor who only played one role at a time!

Q: What went into the creation of a... unique character such as Henry Watson Fairfax?

A: Fairfax, who appears in my story, "Excerpts from the Records of the New Zodiac and the Diaries of Henry Watson Fairfax," was born from my desire to write a story about how businesses and businessmen gobbled each other up. I guess it occurred to me: what if it got to the point where they really gobbled each other up? I was inspired by a copy of *Records of the Zodiac: 1915-1928*, a dining club of the super-rich. Everything just clicked into place, and I had a great deal of fun working out the menus for each meal, as they got more and complex and, um, expensive.

Q: With *Siege of Stone*, the Searchers series ends. Will you ever go back to that world?

A: Very doubtful. It was quite unlike me to do a series in the first place, but I did so at the request of a publisher. I see the Searchers series, however, as one long novel in three parts rather than a series. Due to terrible covers on the original paperbacks, and a lack of promised promotion on the publishers' part, each book sold fewer copies than the one before (and since they cut the print run on each subsequent volume, that was a self-fulfilling prophecy).

Q: *Ash Wednesday* was reissued in ebook format, containing material that was not used in the original publication. What happened that led the original publisher to want a different ending?

A: David Hartwell was the editor of the book, and he felt that it should end with what he referred to as the birth screams of a new world. I preferred to end with the more thoughtful and quieter final chapter, which resolves, at least metaphysically, the main questions, but bowed to David's judgment, especially since it (and Soulstorm) were my first book deal. Later on I might have dug in my heels. I thought it was too much of a horror movie shock ending, and some critics felt that way as well. Still, the book was well received and is considered a minor classic today. I did have the final chapter printed in Footsteps, a fanzine, and it now appears in the ebook, back where I always felt it belongs.

Q: *Ash Wednesday* also uses the ghostly characters as embodiments of sin occurring in the physical plane of existence. Is Horror best suited for that kind of moral mirror?

A: I really think it is. I've never written horror just to scare. That's too easy to do. I always feel that if I haven't provided a deeper subtext of some sort, I've failed. There has to be something for the reader to take away and think about other than just frightening or horrific scenes. If you read my short story collection, *Figures in Rain*, (now available as an ebook, much less expensive than the Ash-Tree Press hardcover), you'll find a wide array of stories dealing with moral ambiguity (as well as some good scares, of course!). I think ghost stories in particular provide great opportunities for metaphor.

Q: How did *Soulstorm* come to be? How did you keep the haunted house theme tense yet subtle?

A: *Soulstorm* was my first novel, and, as such, I wanted to work within a relatively small canvas. I've always been a fan of good haunted house novels, like *The Haunting of Hill House*, *Hell House*, and *The Shining*, so I figured that the scenario was perfect, with a small cast of characters in a limited environment. I tried to make the horror in the story as much psychological as overt, which I think helps contribute to the tension.

Q: Robert Bloch, author of Psycho said about *Soulstorm;* "Williamson has written a real chiller…an enchanting evocation of evil…Crammed with weird insights into a terrifying supernatural intelligence and moments of literally monstrous murder that will make your old nightmares seem tepid and drab." How does such praise effect you?

A: Bloch was one of my primary influences, so having those words come from him was quite nice. One of the great things about starting out was having some of those writers who I grew up reading saying good things about my work. I recall Fritz Leiber praised *Ash Wednesday* in Locus, and to me he was a giant, so those things mean a lot, and spur you to try and do good work.

Q: Zombies or vampires?

A: Neither. I'm bloody sick to death of both. I think horror writers should agree to put both vampires and zombies in the "To Be Revisited at a Later Date" pile. But then that would eliminate about 97.6% of all the horror being written and published (and mostly self-published) today. And that would be a good thing.

Q: What are you working on now?

A: I'm halfway into a noir novel set in 1953. It deals with lust, crime, heroin, betrayal, and a very special semi-supernatural talent. It's something different for me, and I'm enjoying the hell out of it even as it occasionally drives me insane. And there's not a zombie nor a vampire in sight.

Q: Anything you'd like your fans to know?

A: Just that most of my backlist is in print from Crossroad Press and in the Kindle Store, as well as all other ebook stores. *Defenders of the Faith*, a horrific suspense novel, is my newest print book, also at Amazon. Folks can friend me on Facebook and follow me on Twitter (I'm @chetwill). Thanks!

NANCY KRESS

Nancy began writing in 1976 but has achieved her greatest notice since the publication of her Hugo and Nebula-winning 1991 novella *Beggars in Spain* which was later expanded into a novel with the same title. In addition to her novels, Kress has written numerous short stories and is a regular columnist for Writer's Digest. She is a regular at Clarion writing workshops and at The Writers Center in Bethesda, Maryland. During the winter of 2008/09, Nancy Kress was the Picador Guest Professor for Literature at the University of Leipzig's Institute for American Studies in Leipzig, Germany.

In Interspace, her blog is nancykressblogspot.com

Q: As a writer of both Science Fiction and Fantasy, do either one have a particular appeal?

A: They have different appeals. SF requires more logical thinking, as one extrapolates from where we are now—technologically, socially—to where the story is going to be set. With fantasy, the appeal is letting one's mind go free of the present and devise settings and situations that don't have to be related as much to here and now. For both, however, I think that the characters are what matter the most. People are not following George R.R. Martin's *Game of Thrones* because of the War-of-Roses setting, but for Tyrion, Daenerys, and the rest,

Q: Were there any female authors that influenced either your dynamic style or simply your decision to write? Was there even a distinction between female and male authors?

A: Ursula Le Guinn had an enormous effect on me. Not because I write like her, but because she represents for me the ideal blending of character, idea, plot, and that lovely and eloquent prose.

Q: Do you see the advent of e-books and the glut of self-publishing to be perhaps the mid-list?

A: Right now, self-published e-books are turning the Internet into one gigantic slush pile, with readers not knowing if a book by an unknown is good or not until they buy it. Previously, editors filtered the glut by what they chose to publish. It's the Wild West out there now, and nobody knows how it will settle out. Personally, I love my Kindle and both read on it constantly and am making my own backlist available in e-form.

Q: Do you think that e-readers will allow for more people to (God forbid) embrace reading as a primary source of entertainment?

A: No. People who always read, will continue to read. Those who don't read, won't. It's not the medium that determines that; it's the personality.

Q: You've said that in your story "Fountain of Age," you discovered your inner criminal. What was that unique-sounding experience like?

A: All that any writer has to is his or her own experience. If you've never committed a murder and you're writing a murderer, you draw on the times you felt angry enough to commit a murder. To create Max Feder in "Fountain of Age," I imagined what it would be like to commit cheerful thievery, with no stabs of conscience about it. Would I ever do that? No. Probably not. I don't think so. But... There is Max, drawn out of me.

Q: What went into the world-building of the Beggar's Trilogy?

A: For years I had read two writers with opposite thinking about economics—Ursula Le Guin's ethical anarchy in *The Dispossessed*, and Ayn Rand's Libertarian Objectivism. Neither seemed plausible to me; that was one strand contributing to *Beggars In Spain*. I need a lot of sleep and envy those who do not; that was another strand. Who knows what else? My world-building is partly intuitive, and pieces of one's own life, sometimes disguised and sometimes not, end up in one's novels.

Q: *Beggars in Spain* won both the Hugo and Nebula awards. What sort of effect did that have on your writing?

A: None. Writing goes forward despite awards, stalls despite awards, turns out well or not despite awards. The Hugo and Nebula had an effect on my emotions, however—it's sweet to have validation that other people like the stories one is offering.

Q: Your work in Science Fiction has the thread of humanism with the confines of technology. Is that something that was an intentional theme?

A: I think all SF has that theme, in that it has characters ('humanism") and technology, whether the tech is spaceships, future weapons, biotech, time travel devices, or the discovery of fire.

Q: *After the Fall, Before the Fall, During the Fall* is your latest novel to date; what can your readers expect from it?

A: The book, which is actually a novella (38,000 words), is about survival. The story moves back and forth between present day and a future in which much of the Earth has been destroyed, and everybody is mistaken about who did it. There are aliens, adolescents, FBI, and one of my own favorite characters, Pete, whom the reviewer on Tor.com calls "heartbreaking and unforgettable." I hope readers find this one, because I think it's one of the best things I've written in a while (not that the author is always a reliable judge!)

Q: You've also written about the act of fiction writing in your book *Elements of Fiction Writing and Dynamic Characters*. What made you throw your hat in that particular ring?

A: For sixteen years I wrote a column on writing fiction for *Writers Digest* magazine. My three books on writing grew out of my columns.

Q: Given the choice, would you rather eat dessert first?

A: No. I believe in delayed gratification, and in the joys of anticipation. A good crème brulée deserves to make a grand entrance at the end.

MIKE RESNICK

According to Locus, Mike is the all-time leading award winner, living or dead, for short science fiction. He is the winner of five Hugos, a Nebula, and other major awards in the United States, France, Spain, Japan, Croatia and Poland. He is the author of 68 novels, over 250 stories, and 2 screenplays, and is the editor of 41 anthologies. His work has been translated into 25 languages. He was the Guest of Honor at the 2012 Worldcon.

Mike can be found online as @ResnickMike on Twitter or at www.mikeresnick.com.

Q: How did the Lucifer Jones stories come to be?

A: Lucifer Jones was born one evening back in the late 1970s. I was trading videotapes with a number of other people—stores hadn't started renting them yet, and this was the only way to increase your collection at anything above a snail's pace—and one of my correspondents asked for a copy of *She*, with Ursula Andress, which happened to be playing on Cincinnati television.

I looked in my *Maltin Guide* and found that *She* ran 117 minutes. Now, this was back in the dear dead days when everyone knew that Beta was the better format, and it just so happened that the longest Beta tape in existence at the time was two hours. So I realized that I couldn't just put the tape on and record the movie, commercials and all, because the tape wasn't long enough. Therefore, like a good correspondent/trader, I sat down, controls in hand, to dub the movie (which I had never seen before) and edit out the commercials as they showed up.

About fifteen minutes into the film, Carol entered the video room, absolutely certain from my peals of wild laughter that I was watching a Marx Brothers festival that I had neglected to tell her about. Wrong. I was simply watching one of the more inept films ever made.

And after it was over, I got to thinking: if they could be that funny by accident, what if somebody took those same tried-and-true pulp themes and tried to be funny on purpose?

So I went to my typewriter—this was back in the pre-computer days—and wrote down the most oft-abused African stories that one was likely to find in old pulp magazines and B movies: the elephants' graveyard, Tarzan, lost races, mummies, white goddesses, slave-trading, what-have-you. When I got up to twelve, I figured I had enough for a book... but I needed a unifying factor.

Enter Lucifer Jones.

Africa today isn't so much a dark and mysterious continent as it is an impoverished and hungry one, so I decided to set the book back in the 1920s, when things were wilder and most of the romantic legends of the pulps and B movies hadn't been thoroughly disproved.

Who was the most likely kind of character to roam to all points of Africa's compass? A missionary.

What was funny about a missionary? Nothing. So Lucifer became a con man who presented himself as a missionary. (As he is fond of explaining it, his religion is "a little something me and God whipped up betwixt ourselves of a Sunday afternoon.")

Now, the stories themselves were easy enough to plot: just take a traditional pulp tale and stand it on its ear. But anyone could do that: I decided to add a little texture by having Lucifer narrate the book in the first person, and to make his language a cross between the almost-poetry of *Trader Horn* and the fractured English of *Pogo Possum*, and in truth I think there is more humor embedded in the language than in the plots.

Q: You said a few years back that you had wanted to write a Western; Has *The Doctor and the Kid* fulfilled that ambition?

A: Actually, *The Buntline Special*, which preceded *The Doctor and the Kid*, fulfilled it. I'd always wanted to write a novel about Doc Holliday and Johnny Ringo, the only two college-educated gunslingers in the West, and this gave me the opportunity. I hadn't planned to have steampunk, zombies and vampires in it, but what the hell, at least I got to write it and it was a lot of fun—and successful enough that I signed to do three more, of which *The Doctor and the Kid* was the first of them.

Q: Are there any authors outside the genres of SF and F whose work has influenced you?

A: Sure. My Harry the Book stories are (I think) exactly what Damon Runyon would write if he were alive today. Raymond Chandler certainly inspired my mystery novels, and Craig Rice's madcap comedy/mysteries were at least partially behind the John Justin Mallory novels and stories. (Her hero is John J. Malone; notice a similarity?) There are probably hundreds of other influences, but the ones I'm most aware of are Thorne Smith, Alexander Lake, and Nikos Kazantzakis. And Robert Ruark. And Joseph Heller. And, and, and…

Q: You are very much a fan of the genres you write in. How has being a fan affected the way you view books or movies in that genre?

A: It's probably made me more critical of the movies. I recently was asked to list my 100 favorite movies. The only science fiction film on the list was *Forbidden Planet*, which was 96th.

I got tired of having my intellect insulted on a nightly basis, so I gave up watching television in 1982. Oh, I still watch the news, and some sports, and some old movies, but I haven't seen an episode of a network series in literally 30 years, I've missed most of the science fiction series that everyone talks about, and between you and me, I do not feel culturally deprived.

The one thing that changes when you become a professional writer, is that you don't read for pleasure any more. You *try* to, but you are always analyzing. If a story works, you have to figure out why and how…and if it doesn't work, you have to dope out why not so you can avoid that pitfall.

Q: The Starship series has managed to balance a kind of sweeping Space Opera with the asset of dynamic characters, the emotional voice, as well as the sense of adventure. I think that's a hard trick to pull off whether in books or movies.

A: I agree. I wanted to write a military series in which brains were more important than high-tech weaponry. I don't think the Good Guys fire five shots in the first two books.

And speaking of characters in general, when I got into this field I was told that what separated science fiction from all other categories of fiction were ideas, and that in our field they were more important than characters. I thought it was bullshit when I heard it, and I think it's bullshit now. And I can't tell you how glad I am that Ray Bradbury and so many others who preceded me proved it was.

Q: *Stalking the Dragon* is sort of Mystery turned on its ear. Was that the way it had been intended from the start?

A: Absolutely. Actually, that's the third book in the series, following *Stalking the Unicorn* (1987) and *Stalking the Vampire* (2008). And this summer there'll be a collection of the Mallory stories, *Stalking the Zombie*.

It was back in the mid-1980s that I decided, after all my science fiction novels, it was time to write a fantasy novel. Now, I happen to loathe magical quest stories with Lords, Ladies, archaic English, and enchanted swords, and they were so popular at the time that one of my colleagues (I think it was Bob Silverberg) invented the term "elf-and-unicorn trilogy" as a pejorative.

I got to thinking about it, and decided that my novel should have an elf and a unicorn and be the farthest thing anyone could imagine when they heard that term, so I set it in present-day Manhattan—not the Manhattan you and I visit, but the one you can only see out of the corner of your eye, and which vanishes away when you turn to face it head on. It's a Manhattan populated by lecherous elves, incompetent magicians, entrepreneurial goblins, and the like, and boasts structures such as the Vampire State Building and Madison Round Garden.

Q: How did your involvement with *Tarzan Alive* come to be?

A: I got into fandom and prodom through the Burroughs door. I was the assistant editor of *ERB-dom* when it became the only Burroughs fanzine to win a Hugo back in 1966, and that same year I sold my first sf novel, a Burroughs pastiche.

Move the clock ahead a few decades, and the University of Nebraska Press asked me to write an introduction to *The Land That Time Forgot*. I guess they liked it, because not too long after that they asked me to introduce Phil's *Tarzan Alive*.

Q: *Tales of the Velvet Comet* is a favorite series of yours for me. Will we ever see more?

A: No, and for a reason that might surprise you. I enjoyed writing that series, and I have no problem with the subject matter. But each book had to re-introduce the Velvet Comet and, in essence, give you the floor plan yet again, since 100% of the action took place aboard it. And I got so sick and tired of finding new and interesting ways to describe the same damned ship over and over again that I decided the series was finished, that I just never want to describe the layout of the Comet again.

Q: What led to your interest in Africa?

A: Not Burroughs, oddly enough, but a wonderful writer named Alexander Lake, who was a white hunter during the first third of a century. I was thrilled to be able to bring his two books, *Killers in Africa* and *Hunter's Choice*, back into print a few years ago in The Resnick Library of African Adventure, which I edited for Alexander Books.

Q: You are the all-time leading award-winner according to Locus, with no less than five Hugos and a Nebula. Does that kind of recognition help or hinder an author?

A: It can't hinder you, as long as you remember that if you stand right outside the hotel ten minutes after you win a Hugo or a Nebula and ask the first 100 people who walk past if they know what the Hugo or Nebula *is*, you will be exceptionally lucky if even one of the hundred knows.

If you have any books out, winning won't affect your advances, because they're based on your track record...but it'll help selling foreign rights, since you don't have a track record at many of those houses (and if you do, it can probably be credited to or blamed on your translator). The award is a shorthand way to show a foreign editor that you're a class act and a Prestige Item.

Q: What are your thoughts on the state of speculative fiction, in film as well as print?

A: Like most fans, I couldn't wait for Hollywood to develop CGI so you could *believe* scenes in space, or on other worlds. So they developed it—and now it substitutes for plot and character, and I think science fiction movies are as bad as they ever were. I also resent the fact that for the past decade or two, the comic book has been Hollywood's Intellectual Source Material of Choice.

Just as I think that they have no idea how to make a good science fiction film, the same has *never* be true of fantasy films, from *The Wizard of Oz* and *Portrait of Jennie* right up through *Field of Dreams* and *The Wonderful Ice Cream Suit*. I'm no fan of Tolkien, but I suppose the films were made about as well as they could be made. I just wish I knew why the same industry can't put the same quality into science fiction.

As for the literature, some of it's brilliant, most of it's readable, some of it's dreck. Same as always.

Q: How would you like your tombstone to read?

A: Well, I'd like them to spell my name right.

Truth to tell, I don't plan to have a tombstone. Or a grave. My will requests that I be cremated. Same with Carol, my wife of half a century. I'd like our ashes mingled, and after that I don't much care what's done with them.

DONNA BURGESS

Donna Burgess may be a voice in the fields of dark fiction and poetry, enjoys surfing, playing soccer, and painting and has a deep affection for all things Monty Python and low-budget horror flicks. Over the past fifteen years, her fiction and poetry has appeared in genre publications such as *Weird Tales, Dark Wisdom, Sybil's* Garage and others. She has been married for nineteen years and has two children.

Her Twitter feed can be seen at: twitter.com/horrorgirldonna.

Q: Do you have a routine when you write?

A: Not really. My schedule is different every day, so I just sit down and write when I have the chance. I do keep a notebook with me, so I can write scenes, etc. when I'm not in front of the computer. I'm nuts with outlining, however. Some writers can just sit down and see where the story takes them. I like to know where it's going from the beginning. (Of course, it can always take a detour!)

Q: What kind of writing haven't you done that you'd like to?

A: I'd like to do some near-future science fiction and some Steampunk. I'm actually kicking around ideas for both, so hopefully, I'll hit on something that I'll think is worthy of readers' money and time.

Q: An hour over coffee with anyone living or dead; who would it be with, and what would you like to talk about?

A: Either Stephen King or Bruce Springsteen. I'd probably spend the hour gushing over how awesome they are like some little fangirl.

Q: You did a month-long blog tour for *Darklands*. That sounds rather different from what a signing tour would entail?

A: It consisted of interviews and guest blog posts, mostly. I believe there was also one live chat. It was fun, but it was also difficult. I'm terrible at coming up with interesting topics for blog posts, so that was a challenge. One problem I had was the misimpression that *Darklands* was urban fantasy or paranormal romance. Readers expecting that kind of novel were not happy to get a book laced with blood, violence and horror.

Q: Do you see the *Twilight* series as competition?

A: Not at all. Readers who love *Twilight* probably will not like my vampires. And vice versa. I wanted an anti-Twilight novel. My vamps are tough, conflicted and brutal. Plus, my characters haven't been in a high school in quite a while.

Q: The vampire is a constant in the Horror genre. Do you see any other sort of creature that may be just as ubiquitous?

A: I think the same goes with almost any supernatural creature nowadays. I've read stories about zombies in love, harpies, were-creatures. All it takes is some imagination and creativity to make a creature your own.

Q: What attracted you to Horror?

A: I've always been crazy for scary stories. When I was small, I wanted to read the scariest fairy tales—*Jack the Giant Killer, Rumpelstiltskin, etc.* Also, my parents loved to go to those all night drive-in horror flicks when I was small. I was raised on Christopher Lee, Peter Cushing, and Vincent Price. On television, I remember watching the *Night Stalker* (albeit, very briefly). I still eat up horror books and movies as fast as I can.

Q: What led to the writing of the three stories in *Breaths in Winter* and your collaboration with Alicia?

A: Well, Alicia (my lovely daughter) did the cover art. She is an art student at the Art Institute. As for the stories, I think all three of those were written in a continuing-ed creative writing course at Coastal Carolina University a couple of years ago. All the other students were retirees, writing memoirs or light vignettes for fun. I'm sure they all thought I was somewhat demented, writing the things I did.

Q: *Dead Girl's Blog* is… well a book written in blog for from the perspective of a living dead girl. Where did the inspiration for that come from?

A: I just thought about how awful it might be to slowly turn into a zombie. *Dead Girl's Blog* is a short story, but I am expanding on the characters and idea with the novel I'm currently working on. It's called *Notes from the End of the World* and will be written in a journal form, but will also have graphics included. It'll be sort of a novel/scrapbook. Alicia will be providing the graphics.

Q: With Abigail, you have published a short story as an e-book (for want of a better term). Do you think more authors will take this route, or opt for collections?

A: Short stories do not sell as well as novels and novellas. Collections are a good way of "repackaging" your work—then you have two routes for selling a story instead of only one. As an indie, it's imperative to get more work out there. We need that "virtual shelf-space," as Mr. Konrath puts it. The more shelf space you can take up at Amazon, the more opportunity to find readers. I'm also a big believer in the Dean Wesley Smith method of getting out quality short stories and getting some sales from each one of those every month, rather than placing all your hopes on one or two titles.

Q: Would a self-publishing author have any more of a problem selling an e-book collecting short stories, or a single, novel-length work?

A: From my experience, novels sell much, much better. But that can be different from author to author. Hugh Howey's *Wool* is fairly short, but he's killing it in sales. I do believe series ebook sell better than standalone stories lately.

Q: Has technology changed the way authors interact with fans in a significant manner?

A: It seems to have made authors more accessible to fans. Readers (I'm not sure I've sold enough books to call my readers "fans" yet) can interact via Twitter and Facebook, which is nice for most of us. My readers have been so nice, so I'm grateful for that.

Q: You like to surf; what kind of board do you prefer? Any particular waters you'd like to surf?

A: I have a funboard, which is 6'4" and a 7'6" longboard. I much prefer the longboard. Our waves here in Pawleys Island are nice, but not huge, so the longboard it better for minimal surf. With the longboard, when I catch a decent wave, I can ride forever before bailing.

Q: How did Naked Snake Press come to be, and where did the name come from?

A: Naked Snake Press just came from wanting to publish little-known authors and the need to create contacts with other writers. I honestly cannot remember how the name came up—it just sounded sort of cool. With the rise of ebooks, I have renamed the company E-Volve Books, in hope that I'll be taken more seriously.

Q: You've noted that publishing has changed a lot just over the past decade. What sort of changes do you think we'll see in another ten years?

A: I think the need for traditional publishers will continue to decrease and more major authors will make the choice to self-publish. I believe ereader prices will drop and more and more people will have them in their hands all the time—much like an iPod. Personally, I'm hoping for some sort of color e-ink technology. I love my Kindle Fire to death, but I can't read it outside in the sunshine.

Q: Anything planned for the future?

A: There's *Notes from the End of the World* (*Dead Girl's Blog*) and hopefully, a Southern paranormal novel out before the end of 2012. Plus, a few short stories.

Thanks for having me, Cristopher. Cheers!

ROGER PRICE

Roger was an English television producer, who was also active in Canada. He created the children's science fiction series *The Tomorrow People, Junior Points of View* and the Canadian sketch comedy *You Can't Do That on Television*, which became hugely successful on Nickelodeon in the United States. Roger isn't known for his interest in participating in interviews. Luckily, he made me look good. Now retired, he lives in France.

Q: In television, British Science Fiction has, in addition to *The Tomorrow People*, given us fare as *Dr. Who, Blake's 7*, and *Red Dwarf*. How does English Science Fiction differ from American Science Fiction?

A: Much lower budgets and less time to shoot.

Q: Were there any particular influences you took while developing The Tomorrow People?

A: *Slan* by A.E Van Voigt. *The City and The Stars* by Arthur C. Clarke. *The Midwich Cuckoos*—British film of the early 1960's. *Journey into Space*; a BBC radio series in the 1950's. Dreams of freedom during miserable nights and days incarcerated in a British Boarding school.

Q: What led to the decision of re-imagining the series in the '90s?

A: Persistent pestering by Gerry Laybourne. I never wanted it back.

Q: The original characters returned in the radio plays from '01-'07. Why did you go back to those characters?

A: What radio plays? First that I've heard about it. Is that my lawyer calling me back?

Q: I understand that the original idea for the ending of Season Three was to kill off the leads on the show, but was never filmed. Can you tell us how the heroes would have died? Do you look back and still think it would be best to kill them off?

A: The original idea for the ending of every series was to kill them off. I always wrote a scene in which they perished gruesomely. It was therapeutic. I think in series three I left the pages in the screenplays until the first read through as a joke. It may have been that we were doing the read through on April 1st. I don't know. So the legend started.

Sometimes I wrote those endings to spook Thames TV Executives as it was one of their most successful series. In the end they had to let me do comedy series as well, just to stay sane.

And obviously that was a precursor of *You Can't Do That on Television!* My job was to produce and direct television shows. I started when I was 21 years old with a raw and gritty film series about a gang of semi delinquent kids in the east end of London.

Q: Season Six saw changes in not only the jaunting belts, but a new Lab set. Was there a particular reason for these changes?

A: The old stuff got destroyed in a fire, not much of a fire but the sprinklers went off and the fire fighters sprayed everything. Maybe they also stole the jaunting belts and the Stun Guns. Quite probably.

Q: *The Tomorrow People* took a creepy, almost surreal turn with "The Living Skins." What was the inspiration behind that particularly different arc?

A: It was a half baked satire on the fashion industry.

Q: Who or what were your main competitors during the original run or the show?

A: Whatever the BBC put up against us. They always tried to schedule something strong. There were only 3 TV channels in the UK at the time, ours and 2 BBC ones. They had the cards stacked in their favor and much more money (public money), but we always won the ratings battle.

Q: Do you enjoy any particular Science Fiction these days?

A: No. And I have not been big on science fiction since I left my teenage years behind. I was Thames TV producer/director/writer (So it said on the contract) and I was asked (told) to come up with an answer to *Dr Who*. At the time he was being played by the BBC as a sort of benevolent old wizard. He was old so I went with youngsters. *Dr Who* famously had a Police Telephone Box because they could not afford to build a space ship. We had even worse budgetary constraints. *The Tomorrow People* was an assignment. I carried it out to the best of my ability.

Q: The *TP* novel *The Visitor* differs in several points from what the series became. Were you pleased with how the changes played out for the TV series?

A: I made the TV series. It was my responsibility. That book and others were written after the series had started and as part of the deal and published by the publishing wing of Independent TV in Britain. They would have preferred all the books to be different. I didn't have the time. I was allocated (By Thames) two weeks to write each book.

Q: With the radio series, many of the original television cast were brought back in to reprise their roles. Were you satisfied with how that went, and would you have liked to see any other regulars return for the show as well?

A: I have never heard it. But I was only joking about the lawyer. I knew about it, but only after the event, and it was okay by me *if* the old cast wanted to come together and do it. I would not have agreed otherwise. Or I would have sued except Nick Young pacified me.

Q: Are there plans to make the TP novels more readily available to the US?

A: Would they sell? Show a publisher the smell of money and they may be published, otherwise not. Even science fiction is a business. I know that sort of thing always comes as a shock to fans. But it's true.

Q: What do you like to do in your spare time?

A: Walk my dog, mostly, see the grandchildren, work around the garden and fields, occasionally play with my model railroad layout and or video it. Sometimes I make amateur videos for my model railroad club.

Q: Would you have any interest in continuing TP in a novel form or comic?

A: No. There was a comic strip in the 1970s, which I wrote the scripts for until it became just too much effort. There were also several books at the same time, I forget how many. You can still find them on Amazon.

Q: I have recently realized that in my fiction, there is some aspect of poetic reference in most of what I write, whether as subtext or not and that the "Doomsday Men" story arc with TIM and John reciting Siegfried Sassoon's "Base Details" could very well have been the start of it. Was the poem something that occurred to you during the creative process or had you been looking for a way to use it?

A: Hey, you're getting out of my depth here. I was a TV Producer; you know one of those selected by IQ test—If you score in double figures you're way too interlekshull. Famous for having the intellectual capacity of a woodlouse and the attention span of a gnat.

I got one of these literary questions from a BBC interviewer once and I'm afraid I said "Books are for writing, not reading." Having said that I did like poetry. It's about the only thing I ever won a prize for at school, about the only prize I ever won anywhere. My Principal (The Herr Direktor) underlined one phrase in the prize book. He said it was me: *Ein Kind mit Augen auch, die lustig lachen*—a child with laughing eyes. But I never wrote poetry in English. When I was sent to boarding school in Britain "To learn to speak your own bloody language" as my father put it, the teachers encouraged me to write humor, even directed me towards writing for TV. One got me a typewriter because my handwriting was so bad. So yeah, whatever that poem was it probably did influence me for a bit. But those poems that stay with me into old age are all in German.

Q: Are there any particular *TP* episode you are especially proud of?

A: Yes, but I forget the title, along with I also forgot why I came upstairs just now. After Thames TV let me make comedy shows, which later turned into *You Can't Do That on Television*. The *TP* stories ceased to be silly and became quite satisfyingly dark. My favorite was probably "The Dirtiest Business", but there was also another where the British military start to kidnap Tomorrow People. I forget the title of that one. God that was sinister.

Q: Bringing up "The Dirtiest Business," it was certainly one of the darker shows as *The Tomorrow People* went on. It looked as if when the plots became more serious, the change was global in production; writing, directing, and cinematography all seemed to be especially sharp all at once. Was that intentional or just the way the cards fell, so to speak?

A: Of course that road led eventually to *You Can't Do That on Television!* And that was the end of *The Tomorrow People*. I don't know why I went though, I already had *You Can't Be Serious* at Thames which was *YCDTOTV* in all but accents and name. Even had the slime. And the kids were fantastic. Well Nigel was one of the Tomorrow People. We did have one conflict with him and another with Mike when I had them in one studio doing comedy and the Tomorrow People needed them in the other fighting aliens or bad guys or something. That needed some fast costume changes and lost lunch breaks, poor little buggers. But when I got my claws into a kid I was reluctant to let go. They were in everything I made. Mike was at one time in three series at once. And he had pop concerts to perform. Look for the Victorian Child chimney sweeps on *Horrible Histories* on YouTube. My daughter says I was The Shouty Man.

Q: Roger, I thank you for granting this rare interview. Is there anything you'd like to say to your fans in parting?

A: When I was about 12 years old and listening to lots of radio drama serials all the ones that I liked ended with the same announcement. "Written and produced by Charles Chilton" So I wrote to him at the BBC asking how I could become a radio writer producer like him. He wrote back saying that if I was only 12 I did not want to become a radio producer I wanted to become a TV producer, as that was where the future lay. So I found a friend's granny who had a TV and studied it. TV sets were rare in Britain in those days. I thought the children's TV aimed at my age group was boring patronizing crap, while the radio shows like *Riders of the Range* and *Journey into Space* as well as *The Goon Show* were fantastic. I decided that when I grew up I would try to bring the imagination stimulating magic of radio to television.

Always try to achieve your childhood dreams.

Did you know that *Tomorrow People* actor Mike Holoway also worked as a comedy actor and prototype for Justin Bieber in the 1970s?

It was a business. What more can I say?

CHARLES DE LINT

De Lint is best described as a romantic—a believer in compassion, hope and human potential. He is known as a master in the field of contemporary fantasy, helping to pioneer the genre with his groundbreaking novel *Moonheart* (1984). His vivid portrayal of character and settings has earned him a vast readership and glowing praise from reviewers and peers alike.

His numerous awards and honors include the World Fantasy Award, the Canadian SF/Fantasy Aurora Award, and the White Pine Award, among others. Modern Library's Top 100 Books of the 20th Century poll, conducted by Random House and voted on by readers, put eight of de Lint's books among the top 100.

The proverbial Renaissance man, de Lint is also a painter, poet and musician. His storytelling skills shine in his original songs, several of which were recorded and released in 2011 on his CD, *Old Blue Truck*. A multi-instrumentalist, de Lint performs with MaryAnn (also a musician). His main instruments are guitar, harmonica and vocals, while hers are mandolin, guitar, vocals and percussion.

Q: How did you get started as a writer?

A: It's just something I've always done. For as long as I can remember I've made up stories—originally just to amuse myself. I'd write long narrative verses and lots of songs, making up worlds and mythologies, sharing them with friends and penpals. I never really thought of it as a career option until I met the writer Charles Saunders and he urged me to submit some of my stories to the small press market. This was pre-Internet. If I was doing it today I'd be going the ebook and print on demand route since it makes so much sense. But back then there was a huge market for short stories in small press magazines published out of people's basements and apartments.

Q: How does your music and art relate to your writing?

A: It depends on whether you mean my own or that done by others. That done by others inspires me, the same way that good writing does. My own art and music serve a different purpose that still relates to my writing. I think of all the arts as storytelling—or at least that's my approach to them--and the more mediums I embrace, the larger my palette. Specifically, visual art has taught me how to view the world and then translate what I see into prose—what to leave in, what to take out, what to make up. Music has taught me about the rhythm of the language as I put it on the page.

Q: Are there particular writers who have influenced your writing?

A: Good writers inspire me *because* they're good; I strive to leave with my own readers the same emotion I get when I finish their wonderful books. I think it's for others to say if those writers have left a stamp on my own work. So let me instead point to some writers that always leave me feeling fulfilled, yet hungry for more: Alice Hoffman, Andrew Vachss, Robert Crais, Peter S. Beagle, Patricia Briggs, Barry Lopez, Gary Snyder, Patricia McKillip, William Morris, Lord Dunsany, Bob Dylan, Russell. This is just off the top of my head the list could be much longer. I also delight in finding new voices. A couple of more recent discoveries include Ben Aaronovitch, Stina Leicht and Kevin Hearne.

Q: You've done some shared-world novels. How did you come about doing those stories?

A: It's always from being invited. I haven't done many but the one I'm always happy to return to is Bordertown, which recently came back from a thirteen-year hiatus with a new collection of stories.

Q: You often write using characters who have a bit of an edge; they've knocked around a bit. What goes into writing those characters?

A: I'm interested in the outsider. Probably because I've been one for much of my life--at least that's my perception--or because so many of the people I know, now and while growing up, marched to their own drum. Artists, musicians, criminals, street people, the new tribal folk... they tend to approach problems and solve them in a creative manner, which always makes for a good story. And of course *why* they're on the outside is good story before you even add your own plot.

Q: You are drawn to the Sonoran desert. Can you tell us what it is about this place that resonates so strongly with you?

A: I don't know if I can put it into words. I just know that the first time I stepped out of the airport in Tucson many years ago I felt like I'd come home. I've always been attracted to badlands. There's something so immediate about the dangerous terrain and that huge sky overhead. The connection might have been ingrained into me from spending some of my formative years growing up in Ankara, Turkey, and wandering around in the red dirt hills outside of town. If it wasn't for the lack of health care in the States, I'd probably move there. But as it is, I could never afford health insurance.

Q: I loved *Eyes Like Leaves* and its mix of Celtic and Nordic mythology. What led you to write it?

A: To be honest, I wrote it so long ago that I can't remember how I developed the various elements. I do remember that I wrote it back when the whole high fantasy field still felt fresh and I loved every minute of it.

Q: In *The Painted Boy*, there are a number of story details, which thread throughout the narrative; Chinese lore, Santo del Vado Viejo, and Arizona itself. Was it challenging to keep all that straight when writing it?

A: I approach my story characters the way a method actor approaches the characters they portray in film or on stage. Because of that-- once I figure out who the character is—I find it very easy to keep it all straight. When I'm writing from their points-of-view I *am* that character and just as I don't forget the elements of my own life, I don't forget theirs while I'm in the story. So it's pretty easy. What's hard is discovering who the characters are in the first place and finding their voices.

Q: Could you tell us about your next book that's coming out, and the ones that you're working on now?

A: I've been working on a Young Adult series for Razorbill Canada called Wildlings. The first book *Under My Skin* came out earlier this year and I'm working on the second one now for a 2013 release. *Under My Skin* is only available in Canada from Razorbill; for the rest of the world the ebook and print edition are available through Amazon. Next year will also see the release of *The Cats of Tanglewood Forest*, an expansion of *A Circle of Cats*, a picture book I did a few years ago with Charles Vess. I added some 40,000 words and Vess has done fifty new paintings for the book.

After that I still have a third and final Wildlings book to write and I hope to record another CD of original music when I can afford the studio and production costs. I'm also in the midst of getting my older novels and stories available as ebooks. Some of them are already available from Amazon and Smashwords and I hope to have many more of them available this fall including some new stories that haven't been published before.

SANDY DELUCA

Having authored the novels *Manhattan Grimoire*, *Settling in Nazareth*, *Descent* and *From Ashes*, in addition to writing critically acclaimed novellas such as *Darkness Conjured*, *Reign of Blood* and *Into the Red*. She penned several poetry collections, including *Burial Plot in Sagittarius*, which was a finalist for the Bram Stoker award.

She has written under the pseudonym Autumn Raindance and her work has also been included in the occult book *To Stir a Magyk Cauldron* by Silver Ravenwolf.

Sandy is also a painter who exhibits her work in the New England area. She spends her days painting, writing and caring for several beloved felines.

Both aspects of Sandy can be found here: sandydeluca.com

Q: Writing, poetry, illustration. You seem to wrestle a trio of muses! Which discipline is the one that has the loudest voice?

A: They're all very loud, but I'll break it down. At present painting provides my greatest source of income and it also makes up a great deal of my social life, as I am involved with many local galleries and exhibit on a regular basis. At this time I'm not really an illustrator--an artist who creates work to accompany someone else's vision. There are many out there who do that much better than I. If a writer or publisher sees a piece I've created and wants to use it then I have no objection and occasionally I'll do a piece for a friend. But I normally paint what I feel and see. My visual art is very personal.

The writing muse refuses to be silent. I make the time to work on my fiction everyday.

I love poetry and that muse needs awakening every now and then, but it flows nonstop when it comes to me.

Q: In which order did those muses arrive in you?

A: The painting muse arrived one day when I decided to create a family portrait on my mother's antique table. I was around three.

Q: What is it about horror that makes it appeal to us, whether as artists or admirers?

A: On a personal level I am curious about the dark and the mysteries of life and death. I want to know what's inside the killer's mind, what do wicked mystics do and say when practicing their magic and what really happens after we die?

Q: Who are some of your influences in the arts you participate in?
A: Writers: Greg F. Gifune, Kathe Koja, Darcey Steinke, Rob Dunbar, Lee Thompson and Tom Pic are some of the best around today in my opinion. James Leo Herlihy, James Dickey and James Baldwin are authors I read and reread for inspiration as well.

Painters: The German Expressionists, particularly Max Beckmann, have inspired me a great deal. I also love modern movements such as Pop Surrealism or Dark Pop. Shawn Barber and Fred Harper are two great artists who come to mind.

Poetry: Silvia Plath, James Dickey, Emily Dickinson, Charlie Jacobs!

Q: Your novels incorporate the human condition with elements of the horrific. Is this a conscience process?

A: My characters often take over and the process evolves as they speak. I love to explore the dark side of the human condition and blend it with the supernatural. I have a collection of occult and supernatural books I've been piecing together for years. I have magic books bought in darkened bookstores in Salem, Massachusetts and devilish books I've found on back shelves at the Strand in New York City. The research helps to move my work along as well.

Q: What led you to using experiences like unplanned pregnancy or surviving cancer?

A: *Darkness Conjured* was partly inspired by the stigma an unwed mother experienced back in the day. There were several "homes" where these women literally "hid" during their pregnancies in my area. One in particular was said to be haunted, so my imagination went wild.

From Ashes was inspired by my own battle with cancer. It was written while I was undergoing chemotherapy.

Q: *Descent* seems to be the most popular book of yours. To what do you attribute that?

A: It's my longest published work and perhaps the most visceral.

Q: *Manhattan Grimoire* dealt with a lot of themes, not only the unpredictability of the weather, but possession and visions. Was this active tangle of plot threads easy to navigate when writing it?

A: Writing is never easy, but again, the characters helped me along the process. Lots of *MG* came from journal notes. The character Rico was inspired by a knock off purse vendor I encountered one day in the city. Fragments like train rides to and from New York and churches I'd seen in Harlem were woven into the novel. I'd researched old grimoires as well.

Q: Is there another genre you want to explore in the future?

A: I'd like to do some mainstream fiction and perhaps some true crime.

Q: Can you share anything about your upcoming projects?

A: I'm presently working on a new novella. It's based here in New England and it looks as though it'll be my darkest yet.

Thanks for doing this interview. I truly enjoyed it.

NANCY KILPATRICK

Writer and editor Nancy Kilpatrick has been called by *Fangoria Magazine* as "Canada's answer to Anne Rice" and she has published 18 novels, 1 non-fiction book, over 200 short stories, 5 collections of stories, and has edited 12 anthologies. Nancy has been a *Bram Stoker* finalist three times, a finalist for the *Aurora Award* five times and, in addition to winning several short fiction contests, won the *Arthur Ellis Award* for best mystery.

Q: Tell us about Nancy Kilpatrick the editor and Nancy Kilpatrick the author.

A: I'm a rather ordinary person in some way, and a freak in others, but I think all writers are freaks. We dwell so much in our heads that we're not as much a part of the 'real' world as most people. Like many of my peers, I tend to get lost in the imaginary world and forget about the mundane, so dishes, laundry, food even gets forgotten about or delayed.

I love living in my fantasy realms and working to craft them so that they are understandable and have meaning to others. I do the same when I'm editing, but there's almost no focus on me, it's on the writers and their stories and I see my job as being to help them make the story sparkle and then to bring the story ideas together into a cohesive form, the anthology.

Because I'm so occupied with writing, I'm kind of boring as a human being. I try to do things, go places, and I love travelling. But I'm not a terrific conversationalist. I've never been good at 'small talk'. I was shy when I was younger and I've learned to push myself forward and can talk in interviews, etc. but I'm never really comfortable. I'm a one-on-one person. That's where I feel most comfortable, being with one, and sometimes two people, but I'm not a crowds type, I hate parades and concerts and any events that draw hundreds and... god, quaking at the thought!...thousands.

Meet me for tea, or a drink, and I'm all yours. Drag me to a packed museum, or a sports event, and watch me shrivel! The Incredible Shrinking Writer! Ha!

Q: You've written and edited a great number of stories regarding vampires. Is there any other creature of the night (or day) that you'd like to give more time to?

A: I adore zombies. I'd love to edit a zombie antho but there's so much the same about zombies and it's hard to find a new take, though I think I have found one in a new novel I'm writing. Most of my novels have either been vampire or general horror and while I've written a few zombie short stories, this is the first zombie novel I've tackled. I kind of like werewolves but I guess I'm old-fashioned about them. I loved Gary Brandner's *The Howling (1, 2, 3)*, that sort of thing, and would love to see an updated version of these stories. Or someone to do Guy Endore's *The Werewolf of Paris* as a movie, sticking to his book. I also liked *Wolfen* (not the same, I know). And *Cat People* (yes, far from wolves now and drifted from books to film). I'm enamored with ghosts and possession stories. There are a lot of supernatural creatures that haven't been given much sway in fiction and could be. Dawn Dunn wrote an erotic ghoul story for one of my anthos years ago that sticks with me. This fall, I have a new antho out which is all about Death as represented in the medieval *danse macabre* artwork.

Q: What books would you have on your Top Five Most Influential?

A: Well, I generally don't have a top anything list, and kind of hate lists in general. One novel I loved was *Perfume* by Patrick Susskind. Also loved *The Catcher in the Rye, Frannie & Zooey* and the other two books by Salinger. Shirley Jackson is a favorite, particularly her exquisite story "The Lovely House". I don't like commenting too much on living authors, since too many are friends and people's feelings get hurt. Let's just say it's rare I've read a book I haven't found some value in.

Q: To what does the vampire owe its longevity in all its mediums? There seems to be a never-ending cycle of their stories.

A: As I've said for most of my life, the vampire is an archetype (see Carl Jung for a definition) and that means it's in our collective psyche. The vampire has and will endure. One thing I loved doing was editing *Evolve: Vampire Stories of the New Undead*, and the next one *Evolve Two: Vampire Stories of the Future Undead*. Both of those books bring the vampire into the Now. They are stories for adults, not Twilight, not YA, but the vampire that has evolved in literature from its first mention until today, and into the future. These books, I believe, give a good insight into how the undead have moved along with humanity, how we view them and present them so that they remain with us. Anyone who seriously loves vampire fiction should get these two anthologies.

Q: Will there be a third collection in the Evolve Series?

A: No, just the two. People have suggested I do a three, but I've done all I can with the vampire for now. One suggestion was to edit an antho called *Devolve*, but those are the vampire stories that have already been done in the past. I like fresh. As I said, I'm onto other anthos. *Danse Macabre: Close Encounters with the Reaper* focuses on the *danse macabre* Death. The stories cover a range of time and space and place and many are set today. It's a lovely book with superb writing, and I think readers will find the stories extraordinary in a variety of ways and my hope is to introduce the artwork to readers.

Q: When editing, is there anything in particular that you look for in an author's work that you're drawn to?

A: I read a story first as a reader. Naturally, I'm drawn to certain styles--we all are--but I do have a range and my tastes are fairly eclectic. If I love a story, it's in. If I like it quite a bit, likely also in. If I like it but it has some problems, I get back to the author and say what doesn't work for me and perhaps make suggestions for a rewrite. Editing is personal.

A lot of people who slap the word 'editor' onto a book don't edit, they simply acquire. Of course, if it's a reprint anthology, you're buying a story that's already published so you take it as is. But I do anthos of original stories and that means the stories might need work. They also need to be part of the anthology theme as I envision it. There are plenty of stories available about Death but my vision is specific to *Danse Macabre* because I adore the artwork, which dates to the 1400s, and I wanted to present that approach to death, the dead leading the living to demise in various ways, a kind of dancing to the end of life. Get the book. You'll see.

Q: What draws you to the 'Dark Side,' as it were?

A: I'm probably a functioning sick individual who would be either psychotic or a serial killer if I wasn't a writer/editor. A joke. Sort of. I think the dark side is far more interesting than the light side. What's in the light is clear and obvious and very predictable. Think about it. During the day you see all. At night, you can barely see, so anything can be there. The dark is the realm of imagination and inspiration for me. Anything can happen in darkness and it might not be completely clear or understandable enough to explain. It's thrilling, chilling, fun, horrifying, fantastical. And you get to live on the edge, which is living and not just existing.

Q: Is there any particular book you wished you'd written?

A: Oh, too many to name. I'm in awe of other writers.

Q: What was your take on Tim Burton's vision of *Dark Shadows?*

A: I liked it but didn't love it, but then I saw both *Dark Shadows* TV series and I'm kind of a traditionalist. I'm not much of a fan for modern (ok, the 70s in this movie) smart-ass characters being stupid and shallow and thinking they are witty because they are snarky. A lot of films go there. I'd rather have clever and droll, sophisticated crisp dialogue that isn't the predictable punch line. Sure, be cynical and sarcastic, but with style. I'm a fan of black humor. The movie was well done, and as I say, I liked it, though it got unnecessarily chaotic towards the end. I found the opening (set in the past and full of atmosphere) lovely. I generally adore Burton and also Depp, so I was hoping for more but got less.

Q: Is the feminine approach to Horror much different than the masculine?

A: People argue about this all the time. In some ways no. But some women do tend to write about female characters differently. I write a lot of female characters. Well, I guess I write a lot of male characters too! (Laughs). Anyway, for example, my story "The Age of Sorrow", that's typically me. This story is a kind of the last woman on earth and pays homage to Richard Matheson's wonderful novel, and the three films: *The Last Man on Earth; Omega Man; I Am Legend.* To my knowledge, no one had written the last woman on earth in the zombie/vampire (as you view them) plague. A woman has a whole set of different problems to contend with. That story was published by PS Publishing in the UK and reprinted in the US zombie reprint antho *The Living Dead,* edited by John Joseph Adams, which I believe is still in the stores.

That's just one example and I could give you several, from me, from others. Lucy Taylor writes some interesting stories with female characters from a woman-writer's perspective. Check out her clever and humorous story in *Danse Macabre.*

Q: You've written for the *VampErotica* Comics; how did that differ from the storytelling of prose?

A: Lots less writing, for one thing! I had written 3 stories that formed a novella and *VampErotica* wanted to use them. I did the scripting, not the artwork, of course. It was an interesting project to try to find the essence of the stories so they could be presented in just a few words on a few pages. Brainstorm Comics, which publishes *VampErotica,* is doing a graphic novel called Nancy Kilpatrick's *Vampyre Theatre* that includes the 3 stories, the 3 comics, some interviews and other things, and a link for a free download of a song based on my stories, written and sung by the Vampire Beach Babes. It's been in the works for a while, so when it's finally out, I'll post it on my website and also my Facebook wall.

Q: Did you have any favorite comics when you were younger? Any now?

A: I liked Classic Comics a lot, which were the stories of the Greek gods and goddesses and how they tortured and/or rescued us mere mortals. My cousin read romance comics which I saw when I visited her—I always found them weird, those close-ups of The Faces just before The Kiss, or The Faces, Tear-Stained. I loved the Dracula comics and had #1 for many years. One of my favorites was the original Silver Surfer because I related to his alienation—also had the original #1 of that for a long time. And later, I liked Neil Gaiman's *Sandman* world. There are some lesser-knowns that I liked, goth comics mainly: *I Feel Sick; The Crow* (well, not lesser known); *Johnny the Homicidal Maniac; Gloomcookie; Lenore; Writhe and Shine.* These days I don't get to read comics much. I think the last one I read was *The Walking Dead*—love the comic, find the TV show infuriating as hell (but I watch anyway; only zombie show in town).

Q: What kind of work can we expect from you in the future?

A: I've been working on a series of 7 novels, all at the same time—I told you I'm a maniac! They are in various stages of completion. Book 1 is done, books 2 and 3 and about 60,000 words in, and so on. I am also editing *Expiration Date*, out in 2013, more stories of death by various means. I always have short stories coming out. I have *Vampyric Variations* out, another collection of my vampire stories that includes 3 novellas, the longest an original work. Meanwhile, I'm also working on that unusual zombie novel I mentioned earlier. I do a lot of things and writing time is scarce and precious to me. For instance, I teach writing courses online for a college, and I do private editing for people as well. At the moment, I'm attending the FanTasia Film Festival n Montreal which is 3+ weeks so I'm seeing 2 to 3 movies a day and will review those for chizine.com (you can find reviews from previous FanTasias in the *chizine* archives). And I'll likely review some for *Doorways Magazine*, which has a new editor. All these things take a lot of time. And when I'm editing an anthology, that takes a mega amount of time. This is time that I cannot devote to writing. I need to win a lottery, find a patron or marry a millionaire (make that billionaire, just to be safe).

Q: Thank you for the interview, Nancy. Anything you'd like to say to your fans?

A: Thank you so much to book buyers for reading and enjoying my work. I love hearing from people who read my books and stories so please, email me (email on my website). Or better yet, join me on Facebook!

www.ingramcontent.com/pod-product-compliance
Lightning Source LLC
Chambersburg PA
CBHW071451160426
43195CB00013B/2081